# EMMANUEL
## Reflections on the God Who Is with Us

*fr. Daw Egan, S.A.*

*graymoor*

# EMMANUEL

## Reflections on the God Who Is with Us

*Donald X. Burt, O.S.A.*

THE LITURGICAL PRESS
Collegeville, Minnesota 56321

Cover design by Mary Jo Pauly

**Library of Congress Cataloging-in-Publication Data**

Burt, Donald X.
   Emmanuel : reflections on the God who is with us.
    1. Meditations.  I. Title.
BX2182.2.B82  1988       242       88-13913
ISBN 0-8146-1773-5

# Contents

PART II: **The Twelve Days of Christmas: "The Lord Has Come!"**

PART III: **Epiphany: Bringing the Lord to the World**

# Introduction

*"The virgin shall be with child and give birth to a son, and they shall call him Emmanuel," a name which means "God is with us."*
(Matt 1:23)

The Christian faith teaches that every human is on a pilgrimage towards resurrection. After death God will be seen face to face by those who have tried their best to do his will here on earth. It is a consoling truth: God is our possible future and our future is in our hands.

The Christian faith also teaches that God is here with us in this life. We are told: "God's love was revealed in our midst in this way: He sent his only Son to the world that we might have life through him." (1 John 4:9) We are told that at this very moment we "live and move and have our being" in him. (Acts 17:28) We are encouraged to dismiss all anxiety from our minds because "The Lord is near." (Phil 4:5)

When St. Augustine in the fourth century finally came to the Christian faith, that first fact (the possibility of heaven) gave him hope. That second fact (God with us in this life) gave him amazed joy. As he told his congregation one day:

> This is a wonderful truth: the Lord ascended above all the heavens and yet is near to us here on earth. . . . That Immortal One so far distant from us mortal humans, that Holy One so far above us sinful humans, came to be near us on earth. . . . He came to us as a stranger and became our neighbor. (Sermon 171, nos. 1, 2, 3)

The pages that follow are reflections on the fact of the Lord's presence in this life. Some complain that we Christians spend too much time talking about dying and say very little about living. The purpose of this book is to remedy that unbalance, to speak about the Lord's coming to us in this life and what it means to us.

The Lord became a human being only once, but he comes into our individual lives again and again over a lifetime. His coming is a continuous process in my life. Each new coming is an adventure. My life proceeds in cycles of waiting for the Lord, celebrating his new arrival, and acting on that new presence. I wait for him to come into my life again and again. I wait, he comes, and my life goes on strengthened by his new presence.

But then my life changes, and I discover that I need him in a different way. The old answers don't respond to the new questions. Jesus may be the "same yesterday, today, and forever," (Heb 13:8) but I am not. Yesterday I was young; now I am old. Yesterday I was doing quite well living in myself; now I am in love. Yesterday I was well; now I am sick. Yesterday I was living; now I am dying. Yesterday my loved ones were around me; now I am alone. Yesterday God *was* with me, but today my life has changed and I need him to come again with new instructions, new strength. Yesterday I was rejoicing in God's presence in me as I was *then*, proclaiming him to the world through my youth or my health or my love. Now I am old or sick or alone, and I need the Lord to come to me in that new life that has been given to me. I remember that he came to me before. Now I must wait patiently and reflectively for him to come to me again.

This human cycle of waiting for the Lord, celebrating his coming, and proclaiming his presence is symbolized in the liturgical seasons of Advent, Christmas, and Epiphany. We wait for the Lord to come through four weeks, celebrate his coming through the twelve days of Christmas, and prepare ourselves during the seven days of Epiphany to proclaim him.

These seasons give the order for the pages that follow. Reflections while waiting for the Lord are followed by reflections while celebrating his coming and preparing for the task of carrying him into the world of my ordinary days.

Hopefully this book will convey the same message that Augustine delivered to his people so long ago:

> My friends, rejoice in the Lord. Wherever you are on earth, however long you remain on earth, "The Lord is near, do not be anxious about anything." (Sermon 171, no. 5)

# PART I

# Reflections While Waiting

# Wars and Rumors of Wars     1

We are coming to the end of our time. This is the message loudly proclaimed at the beginning of each new Church year. Each day lived is another step towards the moment when our personal rush to resurrection will be over.

Jesus constantly reminds us of this fact of life because he is no Pollyanna. He will not lie to us about the troubles of this real world. He loves us too much to lie to us. His task is not to cover up the sometimes brutality of life. He comes to tell us how to live in a world where disaster is close by.

We do live in such a world. Augustine's words in the fifth century are no less true today: "Through all the world we owe our peace to the sworn oaths of barbarians." (Letter 47, no. 2) We are no better or worse than the people of his day, but our technological skills have gotten better. Augustine found selfishness and pride and passion in humanity then just as it is now. These vices are the causes of our tendency to destroy ourselves and others. We have always been capable of destroying ourselves and those close to us. Now we can destroy the species itself. We can make come true in our own days the somber prediction of Jesus:

> The days will come when not one stone will be left on another. Everything will be destroyed. . . . Nation will fight against nation, and kingdom against kingdom. There will be great earthquakes, plagues and famines in various places . . . and in the sky fearful omens and great signs. (Luke 21:6, 10-11)

This is the world in which you and I must live. This is the world in which you and I will eventually die. And our question to the Lord is a simple one: "How can I live until I die? How can I face death in peace?"

Jesus answers: "You shall not be lost. Your endurance will win you your lives." (Luke 21:18-19) He is not preaching indifference to evil by these words. God knows that there is some suffering that we *can* do something about. God knows that we can at least try to choose leaders dedicated to the good of the human race. But God also knows that there are some evils we can do nothing about. We cannot protect our kids from making their share of mistakes. We cannot bring loved ones back to life. We cannot cure ourselves of that tension within ourselves that inevitably leads to death.

Through all such troubles we *can* endure if we experience love. Sometimes we can take away each other's suffering. Sometimes we can do something positive to improve another's quality of life. But at all times we can care about each other. In caring for each other in the midst of whatever turmoil is in our life, we can help each other to believe that each one of us is held by the unconditioned love of the Lord.

It is hard to endure by oneself in days filled with wars and rumors of war. But if we reach out to each other, we can get by. Indeed, we can live out our days and die with joy. In our experience of mutual caring, we can come to believe that God's words in Isa 49:15 are meant for us too:

*See! I will not forget you!*
*I have carved you on the palm of my hand.*

# The Light at the End of the Tunnel $2$

**W**e begin our lives in darkness, the warm darkness of our mother's womb. We are not afraid. We have yet to experience light and thus do not miss its absence. We are in our very first tunnel of darkness, and we can't even dream that there is a light at the end.

In those first moments of wombed life, we truly are in the dark. We do not know where we are going. We do not know where we are. We twist and turn in response to stimuli, but we don't know why we move. We greedily absorb nourishment without being conscious that we are growing stronger and taking on the form that will mark us for the rest of our days. We swim in the quiet darkness of our mother's loving body, but we do not know that we are loved. We live in a tunnel of darkness with no end in sight.

For most of us there comes an end. The day arrives when we are delivered into the light. We are pulled into the light upside down and crying, and we are scared to death. For the first time we see that we must compete with others for our place in the sun. Once we experience the light we clutch it, trying desperately to keep it always in our lives.

But we cannot. If our life before birth is a darkness, our life after birth is at best a combination of shadow and light. If we are fortunate, we live lives of shadowed brightness, mostly good but tinged with some anxiety. Only the dead live without tears. The unlucky find many causes for weeping because they live lives that are mostly dark, brightened now and again by shafts of light— perhaps from the eyes of those who care but who are helpless to help.

None of us can escape darkness totally. If we live long enough this side of death, we shall inevitably plunge into new dark tunnels where we are sometimes confused and sometimes scared and sometimes feel very much alone. These darknesses are much worse than that first darkness of the womb. Now we *know* what we are missing. We know what light is and we miss it terribly. In our tunnel of darkness we search for the light at the end.

The season of Advent recognizes our plight and gives hope. Advent days commemorate the days after Eden when the human race wandered in exile from God. In the beginning there was only darkness with no hope. But then, as the years lengthened, prophets appeared who spoke of a change in humanity's darkened condition. They proclaimed: "The Son is coming! Be prepared for the coming light!" And so it did, on the first Christmas Day.

The same message of hope is proclaimed to us. We are promised that the day will come when we will be born into the kingdom of light. Just now we are in time's womb, waiting to be born into eternity. As we live through our dark days, our faith in Christ reveals a light at the end of the tunnel. In the words of the Book of Revelation (22:3-5; NAB):

> The throne of God and of the Lamb shall be there, and his servants shall serve him faithfully. . . . The night shall be no more. They will need no light from lamps or the sun, for the Lord God shall give them light, and they shall reign forever.

Believing in this promise while living through our somewhat shadowed lives, we can turn to the coming Son and smile.

## *Family Love*                                          3

We need the Lord to come to us to help us love as we should. When he came to earth the first time, he proved that he loves us. Now we need him to come to teach us how to love him in return and to love each other as he loves us.

We don't need him to give us the *power* to love or the *drive* to love. He has already done that by making us human beings. Augustine says that our problem is not whether "to love" or "not to love"; it is rather about "what" and "how." Will we love earth more than heaven, humans more than God, ourselves more than others? Will we love too passionately, too selfishly, too possessively?

Love is easy to do. Indeed, we can't help but love. The difficulty is in doing it well, in a way that perfects ourselves and does justice to the object of our love. It is for this reason that the song that sings of love speaks a great truth when it says: "Love is easy only when it is done by two other people." I can write about love in general or the loves of others, but my own loves are trapped forever in my heart with no way of getting out. It is easy for a teacher like myself to deal with thousands of kids over the years because none of them is my own. It was easy for a marriage counsellor friend of mine to save the marriages of hundreds of others, but he could not save his own. The advice "Physician, heal thyself!" may work for sick doctors but it does not work for sick lovers. When you are tied up into knots by love, only others can unbind you. Indeed, you cannot even *see* your bondage, much less do anything about it.

That is why we need the Lord to come to us with his strength to help us love well, to love well especially those who are closest to us—our family. We need his grace to make love work, and where we must exercise this grace first is in trying to make our family work.

Our family is meant to be like the mystical family of God. We must treat each other as God treats us. This means to care about others while respecting their individuality. Being in a family does not lessen our primary calling to work out our personal salvation for ourselves. No one can do it for us, and no one can be blamed if we don't do it for ourselves. Each of us must search for the infinite in our own finite way. Each of us must try to embrace God with our own specially shaped lives. This is our call as individuals. Our families need to respect that individuality in an environment of caring guidance.

The family must teach that there is a difference between right and wrong and hold the individual responsible for the decisions made. It cannot say, "As long as you love me, it makes no difference what you do." It must correct when correction is called for and be ready to forgive when forgiveness is asked for. It must be ready to bear the pain when injury is done and there is no perception that forgiveness is needed. It must be ready to accept the pain of "casting out" the impenitent member when this is necessary for the good of the rest. A home may be a place where "When you knock, they must let you in." It is not a place where "When you are perverse, you must be allowed to stay." Even God has arranged a place for those who wish to go their own way without consideration for God or humans.

The love that is needed to make a family work is the love described by Paul. (1 Cor 13:4ff.) This is love that is patient and kind. It is not jealous or conceited or proud. It is not ill-mannered or selfish or irritable. It does not rejoice in evil. It faces the truth, but it does not keep an everlasting record of past failures. Love never gives up. Its faith and its hope and its patience never fail.

With such love we will not be bitter towards each other no matter what happens, perhaps because we remember that we are all cracked. We will instruct and admonish each other in a wise fashion because we will not be indifferent to the perversity of those we care for. We will not nag so as to make the loved one lose heart because, having said our piece, it is up to God to effect a change of heart. (Cf. Col 3: 12 ff.) Paul says many things about love, but he never says that it is easy. Perhaps he realized that love seems easy only when it is done by other people.

## The Lord Comes with Peace                          4

Those who proclaim the coming of the Lord say that he comes with peace. Thus the psalmist sings:

> I will hear what God proclaims; the Lord . . . for he proclaims peace to his people, and to his faithful ones, and to those who put in him their hope. (Ps 85: 9)

It is a comforting message: "The Lord brings peace!" because every human wants peace, and most of us are confused about what it is and how to get it. There are, however, some truths about peace that are certain.

Peace does not mean oblivion. One who does not know what is going on is not at peace. Human peace implies consciousness, and we rightfully feel sorry for those poor souls who seek their peace in the destruction of their minds by drink or drugs or by a habit of "not-thinking" about the reality of their life.

Peace does not mean sameness, a condition where "nothing is going on." Augustine spoke for all of us when he described peace as the splendor that results from the ordering of many *different* things. Peace is not an existence where there is only an unchanging noon. It is a life containing sleepy dawns and blazing middays and dramatic sunsets and quiet nights.

Peace is not isolation, being left alone by others. My peace is being surrounded by all sorts of different people who understand me and put up with me. My peace is found in loving and being loved by those who are quite different from me—those who offset my hardness with their softness, my weakness with their strength, my cowardice with their bravery, my apathy with their energy, my blandness with their anger. Peace comes when I find another who fits nicely into the curves and gaps in my being, someone who makes me whole. I have peace when I find one who will hug me when I don't deserve it and kick me when I need it.

My peace is found in the ordered arrangement of the great good forces in my life—my spirit, my flesh, my loves, my God. Misery comes when I am at war with these forces, when I am torn apart by conflicting desires, when I use or lose my earthly loves, when I run away from the God who has made me to be restless till I rest in him. Augustine remarked that such war is my natural condition just now. Every human wants perfect peace, but no human finds it this side of death.

How does the coming of Jesus change this situation? Scripture testifies to the fact that once long ago Jesus Christ was born in Bethlehem of Judah during the reign of King Herod. It does not say that it made those times or places any more peaceful. It does not say (for example) that his coming made the humans who had denied his family shelter any more concerned about the homeless. It does not say that it made Herod any less frightened of losing earthly power. Indeed, it increased that fear and led to a massacre. It does not say that it brought peace to *anyone* except those who were of "good will," and the list of these does not seem to have gone much beyond Mary, Joseph, and a few shepherds.

What, then, is this peace that is brought by the Lord? It is a peace that comes with hope, the hope that peace will be perfected in the future and can be realized to some extent even now. Our future is better than we ever dreamed it could be, and our present is not as bad as we sometimes make it out to be. This is the message conveyed by Augustine, writing four hundred years after the birth of Christ:

> God has made the human race the loveliest of all lovely things on earth. He has given us the fine gifts suited to our existence here on earth. He has given us some peace, some good health, some security in our lives, some good human fellowship. . . . And he has promised that whoever uses these good things well shall receive even greater things hereafter. We shall receive nothing less than undying peace as we enjoy our God and our human loves forever and ever. (*City of God*, bk. 19, ch. 14)

The coming of Jesus changes our condition by giving hope for perfect peace in the future and increasing the limited peace we can have even here, as we live out our lives in the arms of our loves and in the presence of the Lord. The Lord has come and we are assured of an eternally conscious life lived with our loves in a place of infinite variety.

## Advent Virtues: Self-Acceptance     5

Our faith tells us that the Lord is coming into this life of ours, and he is coming not in some undefined way to an anonymous crowd of humans but to individuals. He is coming to you and to me in the place where we live. He is not coming to some *them*; he is coming to a *me* and the me that he comes to is this *Donald* (or Mary or Theresa or Mark or Joseph) in all its glory and in all its scars.

Before he comes looking for me I am well-advised to find myself. I must find myself and then accept what I find and be prepared to offer it in humility to the coming Lord. I must take off my masks and my costumes and present myself without pretense to my God.

The example of John the Baptist encourages me in this endeavor. John was honest and without grandiose airs. He was free from all pretense because he knew what he was and what he was capable of doing. Thus, when the leaders of the people asked whether he was the Messiah or a new prophet, he answered without hesitation: "I am none of these! I am only John, a voice crying for the Lord."

It is interesting that the interrogators asked what he did and John told them who he was. Probably they did not understand. We humans feel more comfortable talking about the accidental features of our lives—where we came from ("I am an American") or what we do ("I am a doctor, or nurse, or professor of philosophy, or president of the United States, or a mother, or a father"). It is easier to speak about our history or our job than about our substance.

It is difficult to know ourselves. Augustine went so far as to say that the greatest mystery in any human's life is that person's own self. And if we are even partially successful in our endeavor of discovery, the facts that emerge can be frightening. We can become so shocked by the truth that we refuse to accept it and begin to wrap ourselves in fancy packaging to hide ourselves from ourselves and from those outside. Sometimes we pretend to be gods, claiming that anything that is wrong with our lives is somebody else's fault. Sometimes we pretend that we are of no account at all, beings unworthy of love from God and man.

As we spend our days waiting for the advent of Jesus into our world, we should remember that Jesus is coming to us individually, knowing what we are. He wants *us*, not what we pretend to be, not what others think us to be.

Having grown up in a large family, I remember Christmas morning as being a time of pandemonium as we all scurried around under the tree looking for our presents. It was sometimes hard to find what you were looking for because all the boxes were wrapped up in fancy paper and string. You had to look carefully for the name hidden away amongst the tinsel to find the "goodies" that belonged to you. Sometimes you would miss a gift because it was wrapped so fancy that you could not identify it as yours.

When Christ comes into our world to find me (as he most certainly will), I must take care to present myself to him as I know I am. I need not worry about wrapping myself up in fancy fictions.

I need not put on my academic gown and proclaim: "I am a simple professor of philosophy!" Jesus is not looking for a philosopher or an accountant or a mother or a father or an engineer. He is looking for a *home*, and the home that he seeks is me— and you.

We must take care that he can find us, that we have accepted ourselves for what we are. Only then can we present a truly honest gift to the Lord who comes to visit with us here in the place where we are, in the person who we are. It is a cause for happiness. We can relax. The Lord wants nothing but ourselves from us. That is all he cares about.

What a joyful fact for all of us living this side of death! "Jesus is coming to be with *me* because all he cares about is *me!*"

## *Advent Virtues: Honest Patience*    6

As we wait for the coming of the Lord into our earthly life, we need the virtue of honest patience.

The chosen people of the Old Testament did not seem to have had much patience. They treated God like a game-show contestant, crying out to him: "Come on down! Rend the heavens and come down with the mountains quaking before you!" (Isa 63:19) They wanted their God to come to them dramatically and immediately! They wanted him to come to them dressed as a conqueror, not as a "suffering servant." They were not prepared to accept the fact that God comes to humans in his own time and in his own way.

For some, God comes easily in their childhood and stays clearly present throughout their lives. For others he comes later in life, perhaps when they first fall in love and come to understand the reality of a mystery beyond their control. Sometimes God comes to us as he came to St. Augustine, only after we have exhausted ourselves in running from him, after we have finally given up hope of finding peace in earthly things.

Sometimes God will come with a cure for what ails us. At other times he will come only with the strength to endure. Sometimes he comes revealing answers. At other times he comes with the patience to live with confusion.

Sometimes he comes in a dramatic conversion of mind accompanied by blaring horns and flashing lights. Sometimes he comes in a whisper heard deep inside us when finally the raucous noises of our life have become quiet.

Whenever God comes and however he comes, he comes at the time and place *he* chooses, and we must be prepared to meet him with honesty.

The ancient Israelites seemed to have difficulty with such honesty. At first they blamed God for their wandering, complaining: "O Lord, why do *you* let us harden our hearts so that we fear you not?" (Isa 63:17) They finally faced the truth that their separation from God was *their* fault and admitted: "Behold all of us have become like unclean men, all our good deeds are like polluted rags." (Isa 64: 5) In recognizing their weakness they moved towards God's strength. Distrustful of themselves, they began to listen closely for God's footsteps. They began to wait with attention for his coming.

We must spend each day of our lives here on earth with the same honest patience, waiting for God to come in his own way at his own time, admitting our need for him and our own weakness. He is close to us even now. This we know because, despite all our troubles, we are alive and have hope.


## Advent Virtues: Pious Insanity                    7


As we wait for the coming of the Lord, we need to acquire some of the pious craziness that characterized John the Baptist. In his own day John was recognized as a saintly man, but definitely odd. In our current climate of sophisticated materialism, he would be even less acceptable. In his own way, he was a "yuppie" (young unbalanced prophet), but this would not make him any more a part of our society. He would be called crazy and be ignored.

Of course craziness is a matter of opinion. Those folks who hold up scriptural citations at televised golf matches may seem crazy to some. They seem out of place worrying about reaching heaven while the rest of the crowd worries about making par. But in truth, they are pointing out a matter of fact—the fact that golf is not forever and that even "duffers" die. They remind us that once we "hole out," finally there will be only God and ourselves—face to face.

Such characters seem "odd" because they are *too much* in contact with reality. Even the average college campus (despite its professional eccentricity) would not know what do to with a person like John the Baptist. The ragged clothes would not be unusual, but the fact that he ate natural food and drank only water would set him apart immediately.

It would be very hard to find an appropriate major for him. He would be too slovenly for business and too impractical for engineering. Nursing might accept him as a patient, but certainly not as a student. He would be too happy for philosophy and too repentant for religious studies.

A person like the Baptist would also find it hard to fit into the social life of a typical campus. Eating only locusts and wild honey and drinking only water, he could not be your typical "Good time Charlie." He would not be at all interested in sports—the games we played last year, the games we will play next year. He would not care about campus politics—the games we played last year, the games we will play next year. He wouldn't even be interested in sharing juicy gossip about the foibles and failures of others—the games they played last year, the games they will play next year.

We would call him crazy because he would be acting as though he were just passing through this world, happy enough to be here but mostly looking forward to some future that the rest of us "sane" humans could not even imagine. We would think him strange because he seemed so happy waiting for a world to come while not being terribly passionate about the world that is here. Our judgment would be: "He *must* be 'tetched' because he is not 'attached.'"

If not being attached is insane, we need some of that insanity as we wait for the Lord to come to us in this world. We are in fact a pilgrim people. We have in fact not a lasting city here. It is a nice place (in part) and interesting (in part) and worthy of our attention (in part), just like Disneyland is nice and interesting and worthy of our attention. It is a grand experience to spend some time in the fantasy of an amusement park like Disneyland. But to pretend that the Disney Inn where we rest awhile is our true home is simply dizzy. We are just passing through and soon someone else will take up our little place at the inn.

The Baptist saw this clearly, and for this he was called crazy. He waited for God to come to him and to stay with him for a while and then to take him home, and for this he was called pious.

We should be careful about discarding too quickly humans who manifest such pious insanity. The world called John strange, but Jesus said: "I solemnly assure you, history has not known a man born of woman greater than John the Baptizer." (Matt 11:11)

# *Advent Virtues: Solitariness* *     8

More than one-fifth of adult Americans now live alone either by choice or by death or by divorce. Research has indicated that many of these "solitary humans" are doing just fine. They have perhaps acquired that virtue that all of us need as we wait for the Lord—the virtue of solitariness.

John the Baptist is a model of such solitary virtue. As a young man he went into the desert alone to wait for the coming of the Lord. He was not morose in his isolation. He rejoiced and danced as he waited for his Lord to come. He did not hate the human race. He did not separate himself because he was afraid of others. He went into the desert because he was in love, and he needed time to prepare himself for his marriage with his Lord. He still loved his friends and would joyously preach to them about the promise of the good life in the future and the need to get cleaned up in the present. He loved his friends, but he was not afraid to let them go when the time finally came for him to stand alone before his Lord. He was not afraid to go into the desert to wait for the Lord. He was not afraid, later on, to stand alone before Herod and proclaim his Lord. He was not afraid of the solitude of the prison they put him in for his troubles. He was not afraid of the absurd, isolated death they imposed on him. John was a solitary man who rejoiced to see the day of his Lord.

We, too, need the virtue of solitariness as we wait for the Lord to come to us. We need this virtue to stand the solitude that is part of every human life. We humans spend much of our time alone. The solitary elderly, trapped in little apartments, see few people in a week. Young mothers spend most of their day without any communication with another adult. Teachers must prepare classes. Students must study for exams. Married folks find it hard to get even ten minutes a day in deep, loving conversation. The sick cannot make others understand how they feel in their sickness. The dying must always die alone. Each of us must bear with solitude in the course of our lives. We must learn to live with ourselves and in ourselves if we are to endure.

We need the virtue of solitariness to live with our solitude but even more to allow us to stand alone for the sake of principles. We need this strength so that we can face up to what we really are— beings in need of healing who have special gifts that can be put to the service of the Lord. We must be ready to *stand for something* even when there is no one else to stand with us.

The statistics say only that one in five Americans lives alone. There is no statistic that tells us how many humans are willing to stand alone for the sake of the Lord. But this is the important statistic for me. If I am one of that number, then the Lord will never be ripped from me by what other people say or what other people think. If I have the virtue of solitariness, I shall be able to live in my solitude in joy and happiness, like John the Baptist in the desert, waiting for the Lord. I shall be able to die at peace in my solitude. And that is just as well because no one escapes that final isolation. A human may live always in a crowd, but each dies alone, facing only the Lord. I pray that when that final moment comes for me, I shall be able to stand bravely (like the Baptist) as evening falls on the lovely desert that is my life. As the shadows of my time lengthen, the Lord will call me by name. There at the end of this life and the beginning of the new, we shall stand face to face, him and me, the two of us alone.

*The substance of this theme was first published in *The Bible Today,* "Reflections for December–January," 22, no. 6 (November 1984) 349–50.

## *Advent Virtues: Bravery in New Beginnings* * 9

From our first conscious moment we have a fear of new beginnings. Child psychologists tell us that our first years are critical for future peace of mind. If our first beginning is filled with terror, it is likely that we shall fear every new beginning thereafter. We shall fear leaving home. We shall fear going to school. We shall fear falling in love. We shall fear dying. Our fears can become so intense that we live forever in an autistic state, numb before the ever-changing whirl of life. We express in our lives an instinct to rush into the past searching for that silent, confined, but supposedly safe life that followed our first beginning in the womb.

If we are to move forward with life, we must develop the virtue of bravery in the face of new beginnings. In the words of Jesus, we must "pray constantly for the strength to escape whatever is in prospect, and to stand secure before the Son of Man." (Luke 22:36) "To stand secure before the Son of Man"—it is strange but true: we can even fear the coming of the Lord into our lives. We are afraid to begin a strange new life completely dedicated to our God.

Being afraid of the coming of Jesus is not a new phenomenon. Fear was present when he came to humanity that very first time. When God became man in the person of Jesus, the world shuddered.

For example, the relatives of Joseph and Mary must have feared the coming of Jesus. They would have nothing to do with Joseph and the pregnant Mary when they came to Bethlehem seeking lodging. Herod certainly feared the coming of Jesus. He tried to kill him in his infancy. The wise men of Judea must have feared Jesus. Why else would they not accept the prophecy that brought the wise men from afar to worship the child? The scribes and Pharisees (with a few exceptions) feared Jesus because he was too new a concept. That the Messiah could come as a baby was simply beyond their comprehension. To accept such a possibility would mean a new beginning in their thinking, and they were afraid of where such novelty would lead them.

The sad truth about that first coming of the Lord is that there were few who had the fortitude to face such a radical new beginning. There were few who were able to follow the good advice given later by Jesus himself: "When these things begin to happen, stand erect and hold your heads high, for your deliverance is near at hand." (Luke 21:34)

As we wait for the Lord so many years later, we still need the same bravery in the face of the constantly changing times of our lives. We need it to get through our days of being born and going to school and being in love and being separated from a love and losing a job and getting sick. We will need it in a special way when we come to face that unique experience that is our death. Jesus will come at every new time in our lives and even at that last moment of death. He will come to us in death as he once came to the people of Bethlehem. As he was born into their life then, so shall we be born into his life at our death-moment. Even now he lives in us quietly, as he once lived without fuss in the womb of his mother. If we are perceptive and take the time, we can even now sometimes feel him moving in our lives: in whispered consolations in times of trouble, in quiet suggestions at the crossroads of our lives, in a "raising of our spirits to the heavens" at moments of great love or great joy. He is with us and we should be brave.

We must be brave facing new things because we simply cannot stay where we are. Nor can we go back to old ways and old times. Each day is new and will always be so. In the past there is only nothingness. In the future we shall find our everything. Our God is our future, and we must go forward if we hope to meet him. He wants us to meet him. The Lord is calling, and he will protect us in all our new beginnings—in this life and in the next.

*The substance of this theme was first published in *The Bible Today*, "Reflections for December–January," 22, no. 6 (November 1984) 347–48.

## *Advent Virtues: Joyful Pride*     **10**

We have a *right* to be proud as we wait for the coming of the Lord. The Lord is coming to see *us*! The Lord wants to be with *us*! Surely our joyful pride must be a virtue.

Most cases of pride are not virtuous. Pride is a terrible vice. By false pride, we blow ourselves up and pretend to be the lords of the universe. We glorify our independence and say, "I have a right to do this! I have a right to do that!" We demand freedom with no responsibility. We want to be answerable to no one. We want to do what we want to do and pay no attention to the effects. Pride is the essential human problem. Augustine called it the central human sin.

We must avoid pride, but this does not mean that we should deny the good that we are. Augustine says that despair will also send us to hell—a despair that believes that we are not worth saving. He told his people they were not God but also they were not nothing. He told them that God makes no human being by accident. He told them that the main reason for God becoming human was so that he could show how much he loved each and every human being. Augustine said to his people: "You cannot be totally rotten; otherwise you would not be alive." At different times and in different ways he told them: "You cannot be totally depraved; otherwise there never would have been a Christmas." He said, "You must be pretty good because Jesus is coming to see you."

This simple message is the core of what has come to be known as Christian humanism. Christianity teaches that every member of the human species from the unborn to the dying is of infinite value because the infinite God called each member of the human species into existence personally. Every member of the human race reflects in her or his own way the beauty and the goodness and the mystery that is God.

We have a right to be proud as humans because God wants each and every one of us to be eternally happy at home with him in heaven. We have a right to be proud considering what Jesus has done for us. In order to give us salvation, Jesus died for us on Good Friday. In order to give us hope, Jesus rose in his earthly body on Easter. In order to be a friend, Jesus came to see us and be with us as a human being at Christmas.

No wonder the Old Testament prophets sang for joy thinking about the coming of the Lord! Zephaniah saw that Jesus was coming and could not contain himself. He cried out:

Shout for joy, O daughter Zion! . . .
The King of Israel, the Lord, is in your midst, you have
no further misfortune to fear. . . .
He will rejoice over you with gladness, and renew you in
his love. (Zeph 3:14, 17)

No wonder that St. Paul, remembering the coming of the Lord, tells his people: "Rejoice in the Lord always! I say it again, 'Rejoice!' . . . The Lord is near. Dismiss all anxiety from your minds." (Phil 4:4-6)

No wonder that John the Baptist advised his disciples: "Don't accumulate a lot of useless things. There is someone coming who is much greater than I." Luke tells us: "Using exhortations of this sort, he preached the good news to the people." (Luke 3:18)

It was good news indeed, good news then and good news now— news that can make us rightfully proud and ecstatically happy. The message then and now, to them and to us, is simply this:

The *Lord* is coming!
The Lord is coming to see *us!*
The Lord wants to be with *us!*

*Advent Virtues: Desert Wisdom*  **11**

There is at least one way in which every human being is like John the Baptist: each of us waits in a desert for the coming of the Lord. Most of us are *unlike* John in our distress at being in the desert. We lack the desert wisdom which allowed him to live in and with himself, knowing what was truly important in life.

This wisdom is the virtue that Paul recommended to his friends at Phillipi when he wrote:

> My prayer is that your love may more and more abound, both in understanding and wealth of experience, so that with a clear conscience and blameless conduct you may learn to value the things that really matter, up to the very day of Christ. (Phil 1:9-10)

Paul knew that the reason why we sometimes get so frightened as we wait for the Lord is that we are not sure what we should hold onto. We grab at this or that through our life—this love, that career—only to find them slipping away from us. We seem to be surrounded by quicksand which swallows up all the good things we pile around us. The goods by which we have defined our life seem to be sinking away from us. We don't know anymore what is worthwhile, what is permanent, what will "stick" with us as we slide inevitably into our future—and we are afraid.

When things are going well with our lives, when we are in the prime of our lives choosing between untried possibilities rather than remembering opportunities lost, we overcome our fear by simply not thinking. When we get that first good job, when we find that great love of our life, when we return happily from the doctor with a good report on our health, we are tempted to cry, "I *do* have here a lasting city." We concentrate on savoring every delicious moment of our full life. We say, "Wisdom is not in *thinking* but in *enjoying!*" and we hug our love and bank our money and go out jogging. "Life is a *Gas!* And it is forever."

This is not wisdom. It is silliness. It is silliness not because we rejoice in the loves and successes and health that we here and now enjoy, but because we rejoice in them as though they will be forever. There is no eternal "party" until after death, and we will not enjoy that if we do not realize that every earthly party has an end. We may pack our loves and our fulfilled ambitions and our toys carefully into a picnic basket and sit on the sand to enjoy the moment, but eventually the sand will shift and we will be separated. All these earthly goods *cannot* be forever because nothing in this life is forever. Our careers will pass, and others will take our place. We shall be separated from our loves by changing circumstances, by changing places, or by death. Sooner or later our catabolism will outstrip our anabolism, and we will fall apart. We shall be standing alone in our desert, alone in naked spirit, waiting for the Lord.

Can we be joyful then? We can if we have some of that desert wisdom that allowed John to dance in his desert place. This wisdom taught him that there are only three things that *really* matter in this life:

1. a thirst for the Lord and the hope of possessing him.
2. a continuing unselfish love for our human loves (even those who no longer gladden us with their presence).
3. a life decently lived.

John never had much of anything that the wisdom of this life calls "good." But he danced in his desert because he held onto the only goods that last: his passion for the Lord, his affection for his human loves, the nobility of a life of principle.

This is the wisdom that will allow us to wait in joy for the Lord during our own desert days. Those days will inevitably come. For all of us there is a desert plain lying just this side of our death. When we trudge out onto that final desert to meet the Lord, we will take none of our goods, none of our loves, none of our prizes and awards. If we have depended upon these passing things for our security, we shall then be terribly afraid. But if we have seen them for what they are (true but passing goods), we shall have prepared ourselves by grasping tightly those realities that wisdom tells us are forever: the human loves we have known, the Lord we have hoped for, and a personal life lived in a noble way.

*Advent Virtues: Enthusiasm*                    **12**

John the Baptist was a human filled with enthusiasm, with a feeling of joy at the prospect of each new day. Even before he was born he demonstrated this quality, leaping in his mother's womb at the approach of Jesus still hidden in the body of Mary. He was filled with joy at the very hint of the presence of the Lord in his life. His example commends to us the virtue of enthusiasm as we go through our own time of waiting for the Lord to come to us.

Such enthusiasm is hard to develop on some days. It takes real effort on some days to feel good about what is happening to us or what our future holds in store. It is hard to be enthusiastic on a day when you are worried about your life and the lives of those you love. It is hard to be enthusiastic on a day when you are alone and you have no one to care for and no one who seems to care about you. When we seem trapped in "dead-end" lives, it is hard to do much beyond enduring the burden of each day:

. . . wise philosophers whose main function in life seems to be to do the eternal family wash;

. . . world-conquerors with the genes of Alexander the Great in their loins who must spend their day pushing papers from one box to another;

. . . poets and artists condemned to spend their lives carrying the baggage of others.

It is hard to be enthusiastic on a day when you look ahead and see only a blank wall: a future filled with an illness that will not be cured, a future cut short by a fast-approaching death. On such days we feel like crying out: "How can I be enthusiastic when I am suffocated by the narrow confines of a limited life!" When our vision is clouded by troublesome days, it is truly an act of virtue to be excited about present or future.

But enthusiasm is possible even on cloudy days. Most of us at least *remember* what it is like to be enthusiastic about life. Just now I walk sedately, but I remember as a boy the feeling of *flying* down a darkened street, feet barely touching the ground. Just now I search for anything in life that is not a rerun, but I remember as a boy the joy of anticipation as I waited each week for the Saturday afternoon matinees that revealed to me the mysteries of the great world beyond the next block. Just now I search for any interesting activity to keep me busy, but I remember as a boy the enthusiasm with which I could sit on a curb and simply watch the traffic go by. I was an odd kid but enthusiastic.

The strangeness endured as I grew, and so too did the experience of enthusiasm. Now, as a slowly fossilizing adult, I know the enthusiasm of loving and being loved. I know the good feeling of teaching something important and having others understand. As I look back at my somewhat tarnished past, I know the joy of knowing that the bad has caused no lasting damage, and that my present and future gives me the chance of being better.

Thinking about the coming of the Lord into this life and the eternal life that is mine in the future, I can be enthusiastic even though my present life is confined. As a little boy on Christmas Eve, I was able to put up with the darkness and boredom of having to go to sleep while all the action continued downstairs. Although I was alone, I knew that I was surrounded by great forces that were preparing the feast of tomorrow. Though only a little boy in a narrow bed in a narrow room in a narrow life, I was able to feel joy. Like the Baptist in his mother's womb, I was able to perceive that my personal darkness was only a shadow in a world of light. So it was for John in his mother's womb. So it is for each of us. The Lord is coming to be with us in the limits that define our present existence. He is coming to lead us to the infinite possibilities that await us in the life to come. He has come, and someday we shall be born into his world and see the eternal light. Then, indeed, we will no longer worry about having enthusiasm. We shall *be* what the word means—*in God* forever.

*Advent Virtues: Trust* **13**

In our days of waiting for the Lord, there is need for trust. We are told: "The Lord is coming! Trust in him!"

Times of trust can be frightening if the basis for trust is insecure. Times of trust are times when we are not in control, when our fate is in the hands of powers beyond us. When we are very young we must trust our parents. When we are parents we must trust our grown children. When we give our love to loved ones, we must trust that they will not abuse it. We must trust our doctors when we get sick. We must trust our God when we come to die.

Indeed, our faith tells us that we must trust God at every moment of our lives. This side of death we are never in complete control of how our lives will be. In these days the message "The Lord is coming! Trust in him!" is aimed at all of us. Only when eternity arrives will the message change. Then, finally and forever, we shall hear the words: "The Lord is *here!* Come and meet him!"

In eternity the Lord will come clearly, face to face with us. Now he comes mostly in hidden ways, in ways that are sometimes hard to understand and accept. Sometimes we feel like crying out:

"Can it really be true that the Lord is with me in my pain, in my sickness, in my confusion?"

"Can it be that the Lord is present in such a strange way in my life, that he is present in my failures as much as in my successes?"

"Can it truly be the voice of the Lord calling me into the unknown darkness that is my future?"

"Can it truly be the Lord's voice calling me forward to my death?"

One thing for sure: these are not the days of vision. The Lord is not present to us like our earthly loves. We can't take him fishing like Peter did. We can't have him for lunch as did Zachaeus. We can't embrace him like Mary. We can't sit on his lap as the children did. For us these are days of faith and hope, not vision. These are days of trusting in Providence, believing that the Lord will somehow work out our lives for the good as long as we do not give up on him.

It is not easy. Earthly goods are so concrete! Earthly powers are so real, so much *at hand!* They cry out: "Trust me and I will give you the good life!" This was the temptation that came to Ahaz, the king of Judah. He was under attack from enemies inside and outside his kingdom. He was threatened with the loss of all he had and all he was: his kingdom and his life. God sent Isaiah to him with these words:

> Take care you remain tranquil and do not fear; let not your courage fail . . . because of the mischief that Aram plots against you.
>
> Thus says the Lord: "This shall not stand, it shall not be!" (Isa 7:4-5, 7)

In Ahaz's time of trial, God called upon him to trust, and as a sign of that trust he was to ask for a confirming sign from God. But Ahaz would not. He responded: "I will not ask! I will not tempt the Lord." (Isa 7:12)

Ahaz was afraid to depend on the Lord. Instead he turned to the Assyrians for help. It seemed to Ahaz more sensible to trust in a visible earthly power than in a God who could not be seen. The Assyrians did in fact intervene and did in fact conquer the enemies of Ahaz. But then, for good measure, they conquered Ahaz too. They imposed their rule and their gods on Judah. Ahaz was afraid of losing his life and ended up living the life of his savior. (Cf. 2 Kgs 16.)

His fate is not unusual. We always become like those we trust. That is why God wants us to trust him even now. He wants our trust because in trusting God we bring him into our lives. In turning to God in the joys and sorrows of life, in asking him for what we need, in telling him what we hope for, we run to meet him. When in the early morning we turn our eyes to the rising sun, its light is reflected in our eyes. So too, when we look to God's Son in our dark times, he becomes part of our lives.

The Lord is not present to us visibly just now, anymore than he was visible to Ahaz in the words of Isaiah or visible to Mary in his wombed presence. Their stories show us the effect of trusting in God. Mary said, "Thy will be done!" even when she had no clear idea of what that will entailed. Ahaz knew clearly what the will of God was for him but said: "I will not!" Mary trusted without knowing; Ahaz knew but still did not trust. Ahaz said, "I will not trust in God!" and became the slave of ruthless humans. Mary said, "I will trust" and became the mother of God.

These are our days of waiting, our days of insecurity. We need something to "hang onto." If we hang onto wealth, some day it will disappear. If we hang onto earthly powers, some day they will become powerless. If we hang onto earthly loves, some day they will die. If, however, we trust in the Lord, we will become children of God for all eternity. This we know. This our faith teaches.

## *Advent Virtues: Farsightedness*   14

I am told that as you grow older it sometimes happens that you are able to see distances better than things close by. Such farsightedness is a precious gift for us who wait for the Lord. It gives us perspective on our lives.

The story of any human life is the story of a search for happiness and for that peace which brings happiness. Every human waits for the day of peace that will come and never go away again. Atheists and theists, Christians and non-Christians, all want the same thing: peace-filled happy days. The only difference in the Christian search for happiness is that the Christian is convinced that happiness will come in the person of our Lord, Jesus Christ. We wait for a *HIM* and not simply for a *condition*. We want the condition, but we believe that this will only come in the possession of the Lord.

As we rush with the rest of the human race towards the end of our lives, we want the Lord to run with us. And he wants the same thing. Like a little kid arranging its birthday party, the Lord rushes out of heaven to meet us (in ordinary scruffy clothes), grabbing our hands to lead us to the party room, where (when everything is ready), he will appear to us in all his birthday finery. We are waiting for him to come to us in this life so that we can run with him to see God in the next. But for this to happen we must develop the knack of seeing great distances, of peering into that land beyond limited space and time to the place where God dwells.

It is not easy to do this. We are stuck in the here and now. We are consumed by what we need to do today or what we are going to do tomorrow. The distant future frightens us and we put all our attention in the present. We are afraid to look beyond this place in our lives, to lift up our eyes from the dusty earth before us. To do so is to see a world without boundaries, a world devoid of those comforting limits (this land, this job, this love) by which we so often define our lives. But we must look up if we are to embrace the reality of our lives. The Lord himself says: "Stand erect and hold your heads high!" (Luke 21:28) This we must do to face our future and to find ourselves.

It takes an effort, a virtue, to have such farsightedness. We have a natural tendency to narrow our vision to the here and now, to narrow our vision to consider only how we feel and what we want right now. This is the meaning of the Lord's warning:

> "Be on guard lest your spirits become bloated with indulgence and drunkenness and worldly cares. The great day will suddenly close in on you like a trap." (Luke 21:34)

If our present cares cause us to go through life constantly looking down lest we trip over the obstacles of daily life, if we never lift our eyes to the heaven far above us and long ahead of us, we will never see the personal Bethlehem beacon that God uses to call us towards him.

We need the virtue of farsightedness to look to our future with anticipation and confidence. We must have a "high-mindedness" that will allow us to escape the trap of the here and now. We must be ready to fly on the wings of desire, on the wings of love, above the dust of daily life, above the troubles of our times, so that we can see what we are, where we have come from, and where we are going.

The message that Augustine gave to his people so long ago is still relevant today. He said to them and says to us:

> Let us not be so entranced by the past or imprisoned by the present that we close our ears by pulling a dunce cap down over them or by burying them in the ground. Let's not allow past things to hold us back from hearing; let's not allow our present busyness prevent us from thinking about the future. . . . Don't let the pressures of present things so tie you down and impede you that you end up saying: "I don't have time to read; I don't have time to listen." To act this way is to bury your ears in the ground. (*Commentary on Psalm 66*, no. 10)

Augustine is simply repeating what the Lord had said four hundred years before:

> "Be constantly on the watch! Stay awake! You do not know when the appointed time will come. . . . What I say to you, I say to all: Be on guard!" (Mark 13:33, 37)

## *The Lord Comes to John the Baptist* 15

Our faith tells us that the Lord is coming. Our experience tells us that his coming will be the advent of the unexpected. He will come at a time we don't expect and in a way we don't expect. The story of John the Baptist is a proof of this truth.

John met Jesus first when both were hidden in their mother's womb. The coming was unexpected (John leaped in surprise), but it had no evident effect on the lives of either. Each went his own way after birth, to meet again only much later on. John must have had a sense of this destiny because, as soon as he was able, he took himself to the desert to prepare for this second coming. He knew that the Lord was in the world and that someday he would come to him again, and he proclaimed this fact to all who would listen to him. Crowds came from all over to hear him. They perceived John to be an "extraordinary" man and wondered if he himself was not the expected Messiah. They agreed with Jesus' later statement that "There is no man born of woman greater than John." (Luke 7:28)

When Jesus finally came to John in the desert, it was unexpected both in circumstances and effects. The circumstances were very ordinary. One day Jesus appeared with hundreds of others to listen to John's preaching and participate in his liturgy of cleansing. John pointed out Jesus to one or two groups of his followers; Jesus went through John's baptism in the Jordan and the meeting was over. There was no great fuss. Jesus was ignored by most. The revelation of the Father and the Holy Spirit was perceived probably only by Jesus and John.

The effects of the meeting are also unexpected in that nothing much happened at all. It would have been logical for Jesus to make John his first disciple. John was his cousin. He was a young man who had already dedicated his life to the service of God. He was well known as a prophet. With John by his side, Jesus could have had easy acceptance in any town in Israel. All things considered, it would have been very expected for Jesus to say to John: "Come follow me!" and then for the two of them to go out and conquer the world.

But it did not happen that way. What *did* happen after the baptism is this: Jesus dried himself off and went away. The disciples he chose were some fishermen, a tax collector, and some young men of no experience. These he sent out to convert the world. John remained quietly in his desert. His time had passed. He had accomplished his one and only mission: not to work with the Lord, but to prepare for the Lord. This he had done well. At the very least he could expect to retire with honor. But even this was denied him. He was captured by his enemies and thrown into prison. Jesus was saddened when he heard the news, but he did not rush off to be with John in his prison cell. Instead, as Matthew tells us: "When Jesus heard that John had been arrested, he withdrew to Galilee." (4:4)

It seems so unfair! John had patiently waited a long time to see the Lord. He had seen him. He had touched him. He had proclaimed him. And then he was left alone. This "greatest man born of woman" was thrown into jail and was eventually executed, not for some great and noble cause but on the whim of a spoiled princess and her vengeful mother.

What lesson is there in all this for us still waiting for the coming of the Lord? Perhaps only this: when the Lord comes to us there is no guarantee that our lives will be made any easier or that our problems will have any quick solutions. He may come to us in our desert as he came to John, saying: "Hi! I am here waiting for you. Now get on with your ordinary living and dying."

Perhaps Jesus is trying to say to us that very few humans are called upon to do dramatic things for the Lord, but every human is called to live in faith, love as best one can, and die in hope. This is what the coming of Jesus tries to accomplish in any human life, and as the life of John proves, sometimes this is brought about in very unexpected ways.

## The Lord Comes to Nicodemus    16

The Lord had been on earth thirty-one years when he came to Nicodemus, or more accurately, when Nicodemus came to him. The story has an important message for us as we wait for the Lord. It tells us that even though our life may have a happy ending, even though we eventually come to the Lord and the Lord comes to us, there can be a sort of sadness in our story if we spend a lot of years making up our mind. I may finally commit myself to the Lord present here in my life, but if I am a "Donald-come-lately," I lose precious years here on earth in uncommitted wandering.

In the first year of his public life Jesus came to Nicodemus, but Nicodemus was busy about other things. He was also scared. He knew that Jesus was present and he even believed in him, but he was afraid of losing his earthly position. He had a comfortable life as a respected Pharisee. Nicodemus was afraid that he would lose all if he made Jesus a part of his life, if he publicly took the Lord *into* his life. He was afraid that the world would look down on him if he looked up to Jesus.

Unlike Elizabeth, Nicodemus hesitated in *accepting* the Lord who had come. Like her, he had clear eyes, but he did not have her open heart. Elizabeth's child leaped in her womb and she said, "I believe!" Nicodemus believed, his heart leaped, and he said, "Now wait a minute! Let's consider the ramifications of a decision for the Lord." The Lord came to Elizabeth hidden in Mary's womb; Nicodemus came to the Lord hidden in the darkness of a moonless night.

To be fair we must admit that the cases are very different. Elizabeth had nothing to lose in giving her heart to Jesus. She had nothing to begin with. She was not afraid of people looking down on her because no one (except those who loved her) looked *up* to her. Elizabeth is an example of those humble souls who are open to the Lord because they have few worldly passions to clutter their lives. She did not need to change her life radically in order to embrace the Lord because she always lived in God's presence. Nicodemus was more encumbered. He was like that American millionaire who was quoted as saying that "I am a religious man, but I don't have time just now for God." Nicodemus had material wealth, human respect, and a pleasant life. He hesitated to jeopardize what he had earned through his own sweat for what Jesus promised to give through his blood. The "bird in his hand" seemed more real than the Lord in his future.

And so it happened that when Nicodemus first came to the Lord, he spent only one night with him. In the morning Jesus asked, "Will you stay with me today too?" Nicodemus responded, "Not just now, Lord, but I will see you again sometime." And with that he went back to his ordinary life.

Nicodemus did see Jesus again, but Jesus was dead. Nicodemus embraced the dead body of the Lord he was too scared to publicly hug in life. Nicodemus' story does have a happy ending, however. He was given the time (and the grace) to be born again before he died and thus had an eternity to make up for the three years of missed conversations with his Lord in this life. But even with an eternity before him, I suspect that Nicodemus still regretted the wasted years when he was trying to make up his mind. Enjoying his Lord, he came to understand that losing even a minute of God's presence in this life is a great loss.

There is a warning in this for all of us who still have time before us. We must not waste that time. Once we realize that the Lord has indeed come to us, we must leap to embrace him immediately. We must be ready to change our lives and our priorities to keep him close. We must seek to graft our being to his being so that we can never be separated. If we do not, we may not have the good luck of Nicodemus of meeting the Lord again. The Lord will always be near to us in this life, but we may never again have the inspiration to turn to him. And even if we have the luck of Nicodemus to turn towards the Lord later on, we will still miss out on those years when we could have walked with him through the good times and bad times of our lives.

If sometime before death we finally give our heart to the Lord, we shall indeed rejoice in what then *is*, but always with a twinge of regret for what *might have been*.

## The Lord Comes to Bartimeus                17

When the Lord came to Bartimeus, (Mark 10:46-52) Bartimeus did not see him. Bartimeus was blind. His saving grace was that he *knew* he was blind and that he *wanted* to see. As a result Bartimeus was aware of Jesus passing by on the road to Jericho. He heard the excited murmur of the crowd and was sensitive to a lightness of spirit that sometimes hints at the coming of the Lord.

This hint of the Lord was enough for Bartimeus. He did not need more proof. He cried, "Lord, come closer!" Those standing around tried to "shush" him (it did not seem proper to them to have cries from the needy in the midst of triumphal processions), but Bartimeus just yelled louder. He did not care about the rules of etiquette. He wanted to *see!* He suspected that a Savior was near, and he was not about to let the occasion slip by.

Jesus needed little encouragement to stop. It is easy to have him as a guest in one's life. Given the slightest encouragement, Jesus will pound on the door seeking entrance. Bartimeus went far beyond giving encouragement. He assaulted heaven with his prayers and captured Jesus' attention with his cry, "Here I am, Lord!"

Jesus answered: "Here *I* am, Bartimeus! What can I do for you?" Bartimeus asked: "Lord, that I might see! Let me see you, Lord!" Jesus said: "So be it!" and that was that. Bartimeus looked and saw, and rising up, he ran after Jesus into his future. Bartimeus had embraced Jesus by desire even before he saw him. Once seeing, he gave the Lord his heart.

There is a lesson here for us as we wait for the Lord to come into our earthly lives. Before we can *see* him, we must admit that we *need* him. To perceive that need we must realize that the goods of this life cannot satisfy us. The true satisfaction that they bring only whets our appetite for more. Thus, our human loves make us realize that we are made for love, and they give us dreams of a place where we can love perfectly the lovely people that enthrall us in this life. Our earthly loves can help us hope for an unending love that has the infinite as its object.

Our curiosity about the mysteries of this life, our desire for new toys to play with and pretty homes to live in, our desire to accumulate more and more treasures so that we can be secure in our lives, our wish to be respected as a "success"—all of these natural tendencies can lead us to dream of a time and place where we will have all interests piqued, where every moment is filled with new wonders to entice us, where there are eternal mansions to house us, where our security and success rests not in "things" but in the love of an infinite being.

Bartimeus teaches that we must prepare ourselves for the coming of the Lord by first admitting our inability to see him without help. We all are blind in our different ways. We do not have all the answers. We are not in absolute control of our lives. Without the help of God, we cannot perceive him when he comes or give him our hearts as he leads us down the road to our destiny.

The story of Bartimeus teaches that we must admit our blindness and warns us not be tied down by the pleasures of the moment. To see the Lord of eternity in this world we must not be captured by our times. Bartimeus was free. That is the reason why he was able to see the Lord. Jesus must have passed hundreds of people on that trip to Jericho, but only a few *saw* him. The others were looking this way and that, anxious about making their way in *this* world. The Lord of all worlds passed by, but they were otherwise occupied. Bartimeus had few distractions. He was blind. He had no prospects in this life except to continue begging for daily bread. But with all of that he seems to have been of good cheer. He was not embittered by his blindness or his condition. He was ready to love. The paradox of the story is that, in the midst of all those sighted and significant humans along the road to Jericho, it was a blind man who saw Jesus for what he was: the Lord of Light and the King of Hearts.

God gave Bartimeus the power to see the Lord and the strength to follow him. He will do the same for us if we ask.

## *The Lord Comes to Pilate*   18

The story of the Lord's coming to Pilate is the story of the inside and outside of a human life. It is an analogy for every person's search for God and how that God, discovered within, is sometimes sacrificed to the pressures without.

Pilate did not go searching for Jesus. He probably knew about Jesus, but (unlike Herod) he had little interest in meeting him. Pilate's sole interest was his earthly career. His only fear was that he would make some terrible mistake which would deprive him of his earthly heaven: retirement at Rome in dignity and wealth. Pilate was not looking for any Lord beyond the Caesar who happened to be in power at the moment. He would just as soon have avoided Jesus altogether. Jesus was a danger to all that Pilate had worked for.

Pilate did not seek Jesus. Jesus was brought to Pilate for judgment, and thence began the drama of inside-outside. The leaders of the people brought Jesus to the Praetorium for judgment, but they would not go inside lest they be defiled on the eve of the Sabbath. Pilate had to go outside to hear the complaints of the world against the Lord. The charge was serious: ". . . perverting the nation, forbidding the payment of taxes to Caesar, and claiming to be a king." (Luke 23:2)

Pilate left the crowds and went inside to talk to Jesus. Face to face with the Lord, Pilate asked, "Are you indeed a king?" Jesus answered, "I am, but not of this world. I come to bear witness to this truth." Pilate responded, "But what is truth?" (John 18:38) In that inside place, Pilate (like every human) was able to converse quietly with the Lord about this life and the next, about what is and what will be, about the world beyond this world, about the truth that is hidden in this world.

Speaking to the Lord deep inside, Pilate was moved to go back outside and declare that he found nothing wrong with Jesus. But the world outside repeated the charge that Jesus was a disturber of the peace and implied that so too were his defenders. Pilate was frightened. If he acted against the demands of this outside world, he would surely lose all those good things that the world promised. Inside Pilate seemed to recognize the truth of the goodness of the Lord, but outside he was afraid to insist upon it.

He sought an alternative, a compromise that would both salve his conscience and save his earthly future. Pilate tried to escape responsibility first by sending Jesus to another (Herod) for judgment. Failing in this, he proposed a radical choice (Jesus or Barabbas) that certainly would force a reasonable person to choose Jesus. But the crowd chose Barabbas. Then he tried to play on their sympathy by choosing a lesser evil (lesser than execution). He beat Jesus, had him crowned with thorns and clothed in a fool's robe. Then he presented him outside, saying, "Is this the dangerous troublemaker you wish me to kill?" But the world would be satisfied with nothing less than the death of God. They cried, "He must die; he claims to be God!"

Now Pilate was *really* frightened. It was bad enough to deal with a rival to Caesar; to deal with a possible God was even more dangerous. Perhaps Caesar could protect him from a rejected king, but who could save him from a rejected God? He went back inside and asked Jesus that question crucial for any human facing the Lord: "Who are you? Where did you come from?" Jesus did not answer. Pilate persisted: "Answer me, Jesus! Don't you know that I have the power to accept you or reject you?" Then Jesus responded: "You indeed have that power, the freedom to accept or reject me, but you have it only because God has given it!" The message was clear: every human has the freedom to accept or reject the Lord but not without answering to God for the decision made.

Pilate went outside one last time to try to affirm Jesus. The crowd cried, "We have no king but Caesar!" They implied that Pilate could only accept Jesus by rejecting Caesar. It was too much for the poor man to do. He could not stand sacrificing his career for Jesus. He had too much to lose. Inside, Pilate believed; outside, he was afraid to act. He washed his hands before the crowd, saying, "It is your fault, not mine, that the Lord is to be killed." But inside he could not wash away his emptiness or his regret.

Pilate's story shows how difficult it can be for a human to accept the Lord when there is a lot to lose. Pilate did have a lot to lose in terms of worldly respect and worldly goods. He may have believed in the Lord inside, but he needed grace to give his heart to the Lord outside. He needed grace to overcome his attachment to the comfortable life he had created for himself. He needed grace to spend more time talking with Jesus inside. Who knows? If he had spent more time listening to Jesus deep inside, he might have come to understand Jesus more. He might have become more interested in what the Lord had to say about love in this life and the next. Paying more attention to Jesus when he came, perhaps Pilate would have then received the grace to choose Jesus over all.

It would certainly have cost him his career. It may even have cost him his life. If Pilate had refused to give up Jesus to his enemies, there may very well have been a fourth cross on Calvary—

his. Seeing Pilate on his cross, the worldly-wise would probably shake their heads and say: "What a fool! To give up life to die for Christ—how stupid!" But looking back, we who are still waiting for the Lord know that it was the better alternative. Certainly dying for the Lord is better by far than giving permission to bury his body. In living for and (if necessary) dying for the Lord, a person answers affirmatively the question he addresses to each of us: "Do you love me more than anything or anyone else?"

## *The Lord Comes to Anna and Simeon*   19

Soon after the Lord came to earth, he came to see Anna and Simeon. Literally, he "was brought" to see them, since at the time he was only a baby and could not do much for himself as a human being. But since, as God, Jesus controls the course of history, it is not out of line to say that he was behind the whole event. By his Providence he made it to be that they were still alive *when* he came and that they happened to be in the place *where* he came and that they were able to recognize him as Lord even though he happened to be dressed like a baby.

It *was* somewhat of a miracle that they were in the neighborhood. Both were very old, well beyond the expected age for death listed in Judean actuarial tables. That they happened to be in the Temple precincts on the particular day of Jesus' coming was not quite so strange. From the days of their youth they had been frequent visitors, and now that they were old and had no one to care for, they spent all of their time in the Temple, waiting for the Lord.

One may wonder why the Lord was so intent on seeing them. They would die soon and would certainly have an opportunity to see him after death, and in a more pleasant environment than a noisy, dusty courtyard of an earthly temple. He did not need to see them, and it seems likely that they did not need to see him in order to be saved. But he had promised to see them before they died, and so they waited and he finally came. It was a great gift to them. It will be glorious to see the Lord on the other side of death, but it is consoling to see him this side of death too, especially if you are old and know that death is not too far off. It is truly wonderful to be taking a train to a land of eternal bliss, but it is even better if a friend comes to be with you during the journey.

It is a pleasant story for us who are still waiting for the Lord. It is good to know as we grow old that our God is a God of senior citizens too. Perhaps Jesus made an effort to get to see Anna and Simeon before their end because he wanted to refute the fallacy that old folks really don't need to be visited very often, that they are just as happy to be left alone at peace. Perhaps he wanted to offset the attitude of some humans that old people are not worth very much anyway and should be ignored until they have the courtesy to die and get out of the way of progress.

These are great and good reasons for the Lord to pay attention to Anna and Simeon, but why come as a baby? Why did he not come to them as he came to Mary after the resurrection, a triumphant Lord in a shining, glorified body? Seeing the way that they would be in that new life could have helped Anna and Simeon better stand the aches and pains special to the end of this old life.

But when he appeared to Mary in his glorified state, Jesus would not allow her to touch him. Perhaps he came as a baby to Anna and Simeon because he wanted to give them a chance to hold him. They were old enough to be grandparents, but there is no indication that they were, and if they were it is fairly certain (considering their age) that any grandchildren were beyond the baby stage. When you get very, very old, you are likely to be the one treated like a baby, and you are eliminated from baby-holding for fear that you will do damage. Jesus coming to them as a baby gave them the opportunity to hold a baby once more before they died. And more, it gave them bragging rights in heaven. Peter could brag that he took the Lord fishing. John could brag that he stood with the Lord at his death. James could brag that he went to a party with the Lord at Cana. But only a few could brag with Simeon and Anna that they had held the Incarnate God in their arms and rocked him gently to and fro.

It is truly a fine story, this coming of the Lord to Anna and Simeon. It proves that he keeps his promises. It proves that he loves us even when we get old and decrepit. It proves that (if asked) he will come to us at the end of our lives and join us in our last steps towards paradise. As has been said, it's nice to be going to heaven, but it's even better not to have to travel alone.

## *The Lord Comes to the Young*   **20**

One day as the Lord walked the roads of Judea he suddenly found himself surrounded by children. Mark tells us that he stopped in his travels and ". . . put his arms about them and laying his hands upon them, he began to bless them." (Mark 10:16) His disciples were not happy about this at all. They tried to intervene and shoo away the little folk, but Jesus stopped them angrily. He told them: "Get out of the way: for of such is the kingdom of heaven. Whoever does not accept the kingdom of God as a little child will not enter into it." (Luke 18:17)

The message of the story is clear. The Lord is as interested in children as he is in old fossils like me and you. He wants to come to us in the womb and in the crib and in our childhood games and in our schooling as well as in our old age and at our death. The story tells us that there is no time of life that is too early for his presence, no time too soon for him to bring joy into our lives— that joy that is special to that particular time of our life. Thus, when he came to the little ones, he let them sit on his lap because he knew that children seem to like that and feel comfortable with that. It is unlikely that he would extend the invitation to the big horses that many of us have become with age and overeating. When he came to the children, he blessed their innocence. When he comes to us adults, he is likely to start with absolution.

Some seem to live by the fallacy that they really don't need the Lord when they are in the prime of their lives. Religion (they think) is for the old or the sick or the weak. When you are young and strong, who needs the Lord? The answer is: "everyone," and maybe the young more than the old. It is not an easy thing to grow up happily. There is much insecurity and fear. A friend of mine who is a gastroenterologist said that most of her patients are under thirty or over eighty. Those over eighty (she explained) were just gradually wearing out; those under thirty were being worn down trying to find a place for themselves in life. The suicide rate among the young gives the lie to the assumption that the young are fine on their own and need no help from anyone—God or human.

Being young has special crosses, and the Lord comes to help the young bear these crosses. But he also comes to them to enjoy with them the "best" time of their lives, to join with them in the excitement of planning their destiny. No one with any sense would want to be a child forever. Augustine, for one, said that he would rather die than be forced to grow up again. But being young is just fine. It is a great time to wait for the Lord, and it is a great time to enjoy the Lord when he comes. While waiting to feel better because of the Lord's presence, the young can rejoice in truly "feeling good" with none of the aches and pains of the aged.

I remember my youth as a time of discovery, a time for looking into new things. When I was young, I could move freely through creation because I had not yet set my own roots. There was truly "no place" that was definitively mine. I had moved beyond the womb and the crib and my child's room in the old homestead. I had a freedom to fly. My old loves expected me to fly from the nest (indeed, they prayed for it). I had not yet committed myself to any new love that would shape my future. I was young and I was free and I was confident. My future was in my hands, and even the impossible seemed possible.

It is an idyllic memory, but it is also somewhat false. No human has such a perfect youth. The perfection of youth will only happen in heaven. There I will be truly free. There I will truly find love.

There I will truly be at the peak of my powers and have all eternity to make them even better. There I will not be afraid—afraid of messing up today or afraid of what will happen to me in the future. I will anticipate the future because the future will be just like the present: "feeling fine in the good graces of the Lord."

When we are young this side of death we are still cracked, and that imperfection causes us to make silly decisions and do silly things. The Lord knows that when he comes to the young in this life. That's why, when he did his blessing of the children on the roads of Judea, he probably ended up with the hope that they would not mess up their lives too much in the future, that they would always leave a little room for God's grace to enter and straighten things out.

As a young person this side of death, I need the Lord to come to me to walk with me the rest of my life along that hidden path that Providence has set for me. When the Lord comes to me in my youth, he comes not as so much as a protector but more as a friend—a compatriot, a soul-mate who will work with me in shaping a decent life.

When in my youth I hear the words "He comes!" I know that my childhood defender has returned as a friend who wants to share and help achieve my youthful dreams:

. . . an interesting job to do, one where I can return at the end of a long day and say proudly "This work is mine and it is good!"

. . . good friends who seem to care about me and are willing to share the good times and bad times of my life.

. . . and, perhaps, that special love with whom I can spend a lifetime, that special love with whom I can create "family."

Our faith tells us that the Lord is coming to the young. And more, it promises that when the Lord comes and takes us home with him, *all* of us will be forever young.

## The Lord Comes to Zachary   21

When the Lord came to Zachary, he was in the temple praying. It is unlikely that he was praying for a son. He was an old man and his beloved wife was an old woman and they had been barren since their youth. Pious people, they had prayed for years that God would bless their union with children, but it had never happened. Now in their last years, they had accepted God's silence on the matter and had moved on to pray for the things that old people pray for—family health, less pain today than yesterday, a quiet passage into eternity in the arms of one's love. Of course being a dedicated priest of Israel, Zachary still prayed for the coming of the Messiah, but he did not expect that the Savior would come bringing them a child. Now, at the end of a long life, Zachary and Elizabeth prayed more for a little peace than for a little prince. To have children was out of the question.

But for the Lord it was not "out of the question," and thus when he came to Zachary praying in the temple, he came with the promise of a child: an extraordinary child who was destined to point out the Messiah to the human race. The message came by way of an angel. Zachary was frightened to death. Zachary was frightened more by the message than by the messenger. He was accustomed to angels as messengers; he was not accustomed to barren elderly having children. The message seemed to be an impossible promise. Was it a trick of the devil? Could this call to be a parent truly be a vocation from God? Zachary's doubts burst forth in a cry: "How can this be done! I am old! Elizabeth is old! How can the old bring forth something new? We are slowly wasting away; how can we create anew?"

The Lord was a bit irked at Zachary's question—or more by the doubt behind the question. Zachary and Mary both used the same words, "How can this be done?" but Mary was just asking for instructions. Zachary was questioning the possibility. God responded to the doubt angrily: "You want a sign, Zachary? A sign you shall have! Until your wife brings forth your firstborn child, you shall be dumb." Too much talking had gotten Zachary into trouble (not uncommon with us priests); now he would have nine silent months to listen and think about the power of God.

The story of Zachary tells us who are still waiting for the Lord that we should not be surprised by the mode of his coming or the message he bears. When the Lord comes to a human, that human *must* be changed, and sometimes the change is radical. The Lord gave Zachary and Elizabeth the power to overcome their barrenness, the power to have a child. He may come to us with the power to put up with life or to take up a new vocation or to give up a habitual perversion or to stand up and be counted as a child of God. He came to Zachary and Elizabeth calling them to parenthood. He may come to us calling us to love or to stand alone, to sacrifice or to rejoice, to continue bravely living or to die peacefully. He came to Zachary in the guise of an angel. He may come to us through the arms of a beloved or the words of a teacher or the pain of illness or the blaze of an inspiration exploding deep inside our spirit. The Lord will come often through life and in different ways. As happened in the case of Zachary, he may come with his most radical challenge and most unexpected gift at the very end of a long life.

The glory of Zachary was that he was prepared for the coming of the Lord at all times in his life. His virtue prepared him for the coming and permitted him to overcome the weakness that made him hesitate when the coming finally occurred. Zachary wanted the Lord to come; he prayed that the Lord would come; he believed that the Lord would come. Unfortunately, when the Lord finally *did* come, Zachary was slightly overcome. The gift of a child was simply too good to be true. Zachary was accustomed to expecting the worst; the Lord came bringing the best. It took Zachary nine months with his mouth shut to plumb the depths of that mystery. But who knows? After such a period of reflection he may have been prepared to accept without reservation the greater mystery, as yet still hidden in the womb of the maiden Mary.

We hear no more of Zachary after the birth of his son, but he performs an important function in the history of salvation. His story shows that when the Lord comes to a human being, he frequently brings a great surprise.

## *The Lord Comes to His Mother, Mary*  22

**W**hen the Lord came to his mother, Mary, it was an event unique in human history. He came to her in a way radically different from the way he comes to any other human. Still, there are similarities, and thus we can learn lessons from her story—the story of the Lord coming to his mother.

When the Lord came to Mary, he found Mary prepared to receive her Lord. Of course, he had a lot to do with the preparation. He had filled her with his grace long before he asked her to be filled with his humanity. And when the time for his entry into history drew near, he sent along the angel Gabriel to ask for an invitation. It was only fair (he thought) that Mary should know what was to happen before it happened and should have an opportunity to say no. But (Thank God!) Mary did not say no. She said, "I am the servant of the Lord. Let it be done to me as you say." (Luke 1:38) That was that. The angel left, God became human, and Mary became the mother of God.

Even with the help of God's grace it could not have been an easy decision for her. She had lived in that grace from the beginning, but the vision of Gabriel was an unexpected and (apparently) frightening event. It is understandable that Gabriel should need to say, "Do not fear, Mary." (Luke 1:30) The proposal was simply beyond comprehension. Mary in her humility may have wondered why God was so interested in an uneducated, teenage, Jewish maiden. Certainly the rest of the human race (with the possible exception of her parents and Joseph, her betrothed) paid her little heed. Faced with the angel's announcement, she could have reasonably asked a host of questions:

"Why me?"
"How will I explain my pregnancy to Joseph?"
"What will I say to my friends?"
"How can I carry God in my body and not be consumed?"
"What will happen to me afterwards?"

Mary asked only, "How can this be, since I do not know man?"

(Luke 1:34) and was told that her child would be the direct result of the action of God.

That was enough for her. She knew that God had the power to do anything he wanted. She knew also that God loved her and would not ask her to do anything that would hurt her. Her humble confidence took away all her fears. Her love prompted her to say yes, and the grace of God helped her to be faithful to that yes for the rest of her life.

There are lessons to be learned here. Though the Lord comes to us in ways different than he did with Mary, his request is similar. He wants to be so powerfully a part of our lives that we will in truth carry him with us wherever we go. He wants to face our world in us and with us, and in order for him to be with us so intimately, we must give him our lives.

This does not mean that we all must be prepared to run off to a convent or monastery for his sake (though some will get this call if they listen carefully). Christ does not want us to run all over the world looking for *his* place. He wants to be invited to come to *our* place—that place that his Providence and grace and our choice have brought us to just now. If we are young, he wants to be young with us. If we are old, he wants to be with us in our agedness. If we are married, he wants to be married with us. If we are single, he wants to walk with us in our single life. If we are healthy, he wants to run with us. If we are sick, he wants to sit with us. If we are dying, he wants to die with us.

God came to Mary in the dusty streets of her town, Nazareth, and he walked those streets in her and with her. He wishes to be with every human being in the same way, living on the street where they live. We know that the Lord is coming. We just don't know when or how. Perhaps an angel will come to us as Gabriel came to Mary. More likely he will come in a more ordinary way: in the midst of our love for another human, in the midst of the darkness of despair, in the glory of a delicious day by a shining sea, in the quiet of a gentle evening, in the painful dimming of a life soon to end.

We don't know how or when he will come to us, but we do know that, like Mary, we must be prepared to listen carefully for his quiet action in our lives and be prepared to give him our hearts to do with what he wills.

## *The Lord Comes to Joseph*  23

Sometimes the Lord comes demanding great trust of us, requiring that we accept a fact of our lives without explanation or justification. So it was that when the Lord came to Joseph, he came with an explanation that was beyond explanation—an explanation that required great trust.

It is difficult for us when the Lord comes that way. We like to "figure out" the events of our life, especially the bad ones. When we lose a love by death or separation, we ask, "Why?" When a child does not turn out the way we would like, we ask, "Why?" When we are felled by a serious illness, we ask, "Why?" Often there are no answers. All we can do is to accept our situation for what it is and move on with our life as best we can. Indeed, we *must* do that lest our unanswered question fester and swell until it crushes the very life out of our life.

The question that Joseph asked was a delicate one: "How did my wife become pregnant?" Joseph had no answer. The divine answer had not yet been revealed to him, and the crude answer likely to be suggested by gossiping humans was unthinkable, considering the virtue of his young bride. Joseph knew that she was with child. He did not know why or how. He did not know what to do next. Should he give her freedom from the marriage in some quiet way so that she could pursue her special destiny—a destiny hinted at by her mysterious pregnancy? He did not know what to do, and there was no human that he could turn to for advice. And so he turned to God in prayer.

God responded in a dream. He told Joseph that the child was the result of divine action and that he should not hesitate to have Mary for his wife. God stated a fact without explanation and suggested what Joseph should do about it. That was enough for him. With no further hesitation, he confirmed his marriage bond and lived with Mary chastely for the rest of his life. God had a Son; he had a mother for his Son incarnated; now he had a man around the house to take care of them.

And what a man! Joseph is extraordinary not only in his un-questioning acceptance of the revelation that Jesus was the Son of God but also in his bravery in taking charge of a family with such a son. Friends tell me how difficult it is to deal with a spouse who treats a child like a god. How in the world do you respond to a spouse who is *in fact* the mother of God? And (literally) only God knows how to treat a Son who *is* God. God knows, but certainly Joseph did not.

Joseph solved the problem by simply going ahead and being him-self: being Joseph to Mary and being Joseph to Jesus and leaving the rest up to God. God, after all, chose *Joseph* to care for Mary and Jesus. He must have known what he was getting. All God could demand of Joseph was that he be Joseph, and this Joseph did ex-ceptionally well. In the process of being himself, he found a place for the baby to be born. He took the one and only trip of his life to save the baby from the envious King Herod. After living for some years as an alien in a foreign land, he returned with his family to Nazareth, and there he supported the boy and his mother by the sweat and skill of his work. Whenever God told him to move, he moved, but most of the time he just stayed put and did ordinary Joseph things: he worked; he loved Mary and Jesus; he listened care-fully for the will of God whispered quietly to him through the or-dinary events of his daily life.

Joseph's story is truly extraordinary, and it is helpful to us as we wait for the coming of the Lord through the rest of our lives. The Lord may come to us, too, through some inexplicable event that calls for great trust. When the disastrous happens or when we are caught in a situation that defies explanation, we may cry, "Why?" and hear the response: "Why not? This is just part of be-ing alive in a world confused and wounded by sin."

At these terrible questioning times of life, the example of Joseph stands us in good stead. It says to us: "Trust in God! He may not give you an answer that you can understand, but he will get you through and bear you up through these days without answers."

# *The Lord Comes to Elizabeth* 24

Elizabeth was at home waiting for her visitor. She was waiting for the Lord to come, but she did not know it. She expected only Mary, her cousin. She knew that Mary was pregnant, but she did not know who the child was. Her own unborn son, John, was the one who told her finally, by leaping in her womb at the presence of his Lord.

This new coming must have been a surprise for her. She may have thought that the Lord had come to her finally and forever when he gave the great gift of allowing her and Zachary to conceive a child after long years of fruitless trying. She knew (more than most mothers) that the baby in her womb was a "gift of God," that God had touched her being and changed her life. She may have thought that there was no new way for God to come to her, that she had experienced the absolute epitome of his presence in her miraculous child.

But then Mary came to her and Elizabeth saw that God had come to her in an even more wonderful and mysterious way . . . clothed in the flesh of helpless infancy. Her leaping son taught Elizabeth that there are no limits on how or when God will come into a human's life. But she learned only because she was prepared to see. She accepted her hidden God only because she was prepared to receive him. Elizabeth's eyes were clear and her heart was open.

Elizabeth was able to see the presence of the Lord in her ordinary surroundings and was able with open heart to grant that Mary's unborn Jesus was the most important thing in the world. It was an exceptional demonstration of humility. Before Mary came, Elizabeth must have believed that the child in *her* womb was the absolute greatest. But when Mary stood before her, Elizabeth immediately proclaimed that the unseen child of her young cousin was much greater! In the presence of a still hidden Jesus, Elizabeth changed all priorities. She chose an unborn child in another's womb over all else in her life. It was an act of faith, an act of courage, an act of an open heart prepared to receive God however he came to her . . . in the sorrow of her barren years, in the unexpected joy of the child now felt inside her, in the clouded hiddenness of her cousin's womb. Elizabeth was able to see the unseen and open her heart to a God previously unknown in this new human guise.

As we wait for God to come and hope for him to come and pray for him to come, we need Elizabeth's clear eyes and open heart. But it is not easy. Without God's grace, it is impossible. The Lord comes in many ways. Sometimes we are called to join him in a life different from what went before . . . a life fulfilled beyond our wildest dreams, a life emptied beyond our most terrifying fears.

The Lord comes sometimes in a new venture, a new vocation, a new job that becomes possible only because we fail in old ventures, vocations, and jobs. Peter found Jesus because he was willing to move beyond his fishing career. Zachaeus found Jesus because he was willing to take a day off from work. Mary Magdalene found Jesus because she was willing to take a chance on true love. Dismas found Jesus because (perhaps for the first time) he was willing to be sorry for someone else.

There is no predicting how the Lord will come into a human life. Sometimes the Lord comes when we fall in love, and sometimes he comes when a love is lost. Sometimes we can only come to see the Lord when we are all alone, when all earthly loves have gone from us. In the emptiness of life that results, we perceive that the Lord has come to us—not to make us feel better (at least right away) but just to stand by our side as we live through our despair.

Sometimes the Lord comes on a bright spring day. We walk arm in arm with someone we love along an empty beach. There is a warp in time and space. There is no past with its troubles. There is no future with its fears. There is only the golden beach and bright sea, the white cloud-ships sailing across the blue sky, the pleasant warmth of the sun and the fresh breeze caressing our brows as we talk quietly about everything and nothing. God sometimes comes to us on such days when we truly feel GOOD, when for a few precious moments we seem to experience life itself.

Sometimes the Lord comes in the ecstasy of life, but sometimes he comes to join us in the midst of a killing illness, perhaps just after someone has said the somber words: "I am sorry, there is noth-

ing more that can be done to save you." Sometimes in hearing words
of death, we come to perceive that the Lord of life stands near.

We must be prepared to see the Lord in every ordinary event
of our lives and to accept his coming even though it comes with
pain. Christmas is any day that God comes to a human being, and
however he comes he asks the same question: "Do you believe in
me? Do you love me more than the rest?" If we hear those whispered
words in our life and consistently answer "Yes!" then we never more
will be separated from him. Jesus will have come, and we will have
seen him with clear eyes and received him with open heart.

Elizabeth disappears from history after the scene in the first chapter of Luke, but she leaves us with a good memory as we wait for
the Lord's coming. She shows that if we are prepared to see and
accept him whenever and however he comes we shall indeed see
him and hold him even in the most ordinary days of our lives. Our
faith tells us that the Lord comes to us in this life. Elizabeth tells
us that sometimes he comes in quite unexpected ways.

As the day approaches when the Lord will come to us, we should
pray for the virtues of Elizabeth: the gift of clear eyes and an open
heart. We need clear eyes to see the Lord in case he comes to us
in an unexpected way. We need an open heart to set aside our accustomed lives to receive him.

Clear eyes have to do with perception; an open heart has to do
with choice. We cannot choose what we do not perceive. If we cannot recognize God passing through our lives, we cannot come to
love him. But knowing him is not enough, anymore than simply
seeing loved ones is enough. We must reach out to them, touch them,
hold them, make them one with us. We must change the bent of
our lives so that their presence can fit into the curve of our existence. To make a lover's presence effective in our lives, we must
have the strength to put aside everything else and choose him or
her above all. And this is especially so when the lover is God. We
need both clear eyes and an open heart to make God live for us now.

The story of Elizabeth demonstrates what an ordinary human
can do with such virtues. She was able to *perceive* the presence of
the Lord in the slight body of her young cousin Mary. Although
she knew from Scripture that God was an awesome power, a per-

son not to be trifled with, an infinite being, Elizabeth by the grace of God was able to see that her Lord had come into her ordinary life in an extraordinarily ordinary way.

## *God's Love Song* 25

A few days before Christmas Day, the liturgy of the Mass invites us to sing with God his love song for the human race. The words are from the *Canticle Of Canticles*, and they remind us of two great glorious facts about our life just now: first, we are waiting for the coming of a God who loves us; second, it is possible for us to love and give love on this earth even as we wait for the coming of the Lord.

The power of love here on earth is immense. As God sings:

For stern as death is love,
   relentless as the nether world is devotion;
   its flames are a blazing fire.
Deep waters cannot quench love,
   nor floods sweep it away.
Were one to offer all he owns to purchase love,
   he would be roundly mocked. (Cant 8:6-7)

We cannot buy love because it must be a gift given freely. When we are embraced in love, we know it is because others truly care for us, not because of a good they hope to get from us. We are secure because we know that we are cherished by others for what we are.

Love is a feeling of calm. Though not passionless, it need not be passionate. Though intimate, it does not need constant explicit communication. Though each is possessed by the other, neither is consumed. Indeed, a lover's individuality and freedom is enhanced by the expansion of spirit that the beloved brings. To rest in the arms of a beloved is a quiet thing, as close to becoming one with the other as we can make it. The sound of the other's breath is indistinguishable from our own. Hearts beat in unison and spirits join, facing the world now not as two but as one.

We are blessed if we can wait for the Lord in the embrace of another human who loves us. No human love can take the place of divine love, but true human love can help us wait for the Lord in hope. Having experienced human love—the experience of being loved despite our quirks and scars—it is easier to believe that we can be loved by God.

We are blessed if we have given our love to another human because this prepares us to give ourselves in love to the Lord when he comes. Having given ourselves to another human in love, having forgotten about ourselves for the sake of our human loves, we open up space in ourselves for God. Our love stretches our being. We reach out of ourselves to a good that is beyond ourselves. We become bigger as our spirit strains towards the good of the beloved. Just as our heart and mind and spirit, nurtured by memory of time together that once was, can continue to live in the place of a love now far distant, so too we can learn to live in a land of love that is our future, a land where we will walk forever in the embrace of our Lord.

We don't know in what guise the Lord will come to us the next time he comes. Perhaps in the past he came dressed as he was at Cana, ready to dance with us at the good times of life. Perhaps he came dressed as he was when he embraced the Judean children, ready to play with us and hold us and bless us. Perhaps he came dressed as he was when he came to Martha and Mary, ready to weep with us by the grave of a human love. Perhaps he has already come to us dressed as he was on Calvary, ready to lie with us naked and alone on the cross of our life. Perhaps he has come in an infinite number of different ways in the past, but none of these can predict how he will come the next time. But this we know for certain: however he comes he will come as a lover. He will come because he loves us. We know this because he has already given us the love song that he will be singing. It is the song that he set down so long ago:

Arise, my beloved, my beautiful one,
  and come!
For see, the winter is past,
  the rains are over and gone.
The flowers appear on the earth,
  the time of pruning the vines has come,
  and the song of the dove is heard in our land.
Arise, my beloved, my beautiful one,
  and come! (Cant 2:10-13)

# *Mary's Song* 26

Scripture does not record many of the words of Mary, the mother of the Lord. Perhaps this is because her actions spoke louder than any words. She did not *do* theology; she *did* the will of God. She did not try to *explain* the meaning of God to scholars; she *brought* the Son of God to the world.

Her longest continuous monologue was in fact not a speech but a song—a love song to her divine love. It is a good song for us to hear as we wait for the coming of the Lord because it tells us how it feels to give oneself totally to a lover, human or divine. It tells us how our divine lover deals with those he loves, how he affects a human being who has accepted his love. Meditating on Mary's song reveals to us how it will be when the Lord comes to us and takes over our lives, as he once long ago took over the life of the maiden Mary.

Mary sang her song when she went to visit her cousin Elizabeth—a happy circumstance, since an audience insures that a song will be remembered and sometimes improves the singing. As Mary sang, the child in Elizabeth's womb danced. We don't know what Jesus did. Perhaps he kept time (an easy task for one who saved eternity), gently tapping his foot deep inside Mary's body.

All things considered, it was a happy occasion—two glowing mothers rejoicing in their unborn sons and the God who made their birthing possible.

To understand the excitement we need to hear the song and get behind the words to the truth they suggest. We need to make the love song our own, by pouring into it what our lives have taught us about love and what our faith has taught us about God. The song itself is found in Luke 1:46-55. The reflections are hidden deep in the hearts of those who hear.

Mary sang:

"My being proclaims the greatness of the Lord, my spirit finds joy in God my savior."

When we are in love our very being becomes one with the beloved. We grow larger, and onlookers can see in us the wonder of the love that has touched us. The center of our joy is found in our love, and all of the good things in our life are brightened by its presence. When our love is our Lord, his grace-filled presence rushes through us to nourish all whom we touch with our lives. We rejoice because we know that he has saved us by making us one with him. We shall be forever where he is, and we are happy.

Mary sang:

"He has looked upon his servant in her lowliness; all ages to come shall call me blessed. God who is mighty has done great things for me, holy is his name."

When the one I love returns my love, I wonder at the miracle. My need for love is felt as an emptiness that can be filled only by the richness of the beloved. Amazingly, my lover is moved by my emptiness more than by my strength. The beloved has seen my weakness and has come to fill me, has seen my loneliness and has come to share my life, has seen my abject condition and has come to raise me up. The world that witnesses this resurrection wonders at the gift given me by my love, and when that love is divine, the wonder becomes amazement. The gift given is in proportion to the giver's fullness rather than my emptiness. And thus, when the giver is God, the good given is beyond comprehension.

Mary sang:

> His mercy is from age to age on those who fear him. . . .
> He has confused the proud in their inmost thoughts.
> He has deposed the mighty from their thrones and raised the lowly
> to high places.
> The hungry he has given every good thing
> while the rich he has sent empty away.

The enemies of love are pride and self-satisfaction. If one believes that one can do very well in life without love, a lover will never come. If one feels that one does not need the Lord, the Lord will never be found. It is not that the Lord is absent; it is just that he is unknown or not accepted. The Lord is present to the proud, but their pride prevents them from seeing him. So filled up are they with love of self that there is no room for love of any other. So convinced are they that they are the best they can be that they are ignorant of the Divine Lover who wants to make them better than they could be.

God does not purposely favor the lowly or the hungry or those who fear. He has nothing personal against the mighty or the rich. He comes to all humans. As far as God is concerned we are *all* lowly. We are and always will be creatures held just above the chasm of nothingness by his divine will. But some humans don't seem to know this, and God can't do much about that. He can mend the cracked; but nothing can be done for the crazy who are proud of it.

Mary ends her song by rejoicing in the fact that God kept his promise to Israel. One of the sure signs of true love is keeping promises. In our human loving, promises are sometimes not kept. Sometimes we promise the impossible, like "I will never be separated from you," like "I will never let you die," like "I will never let you be unhappy." We promise in the emotion of the moment great goods that we cannot deliver. There are other times when we simply do not keep promises that could be kept. We promise fidelity and are unfaithful; we promise gentleness and are cruel; we promise "till death do us part" and leave at the first hint of "greener pastures."

Our Lord is not such a lover. The promises he makes he *can* fulfill. The promises he makes he *will* fulfill. One of his promises is that he will come to each of us someday and take us home. If we are faithful to him, this he will do. And then, for the first time, we will *really* know what Mary's lovesong was all about.


*Angels and Shepherds*     27


The night of Jesus' birth was a night for angels and shepherds. Angels sang his praises in heaven; shepherds adored him on earth. It was an odd combination. The shepherds were outcasts among humans. The angels were at the highest level of creation. The bottom and the top of intelligent creation celebrated while the rest slept away the night.

Why were the angels so excited? God becoming human did nothing for them personally. Their fate was already sealed. Those who had not fallen were already saved, and those who had fallen were damned forever with no second chance. Of course, the angels who had chosen God had a tendency to celebrate *anything* that God did, but Augustine suggests another reason for their happiness. The coming of Jesus signified the beginning of the process that would re-open heaven to the human race. Now humans could fill up the gaps in the heavenly city left by those angels who had joined Lucifer in rejecting God. Misery may or may not love company, but happiness certainly does, and the angels rejoiced in the prospect of having so many other creatures sharing their heavenly bliss. Perhaps the angels saw that the birth of Jesus was an invitation to others to join the heavenly banquet—that banquet that had been prepared from the beginning of time but which could not *really* get going until all the seats were filled. The places left by those devils who had other business to attend to (their own self-glorification), could now be filled by human beings. The song of the angels was thus a very simple song: they sang, "Let the party begin!" Of course, we don't know if all this is true, but it is a nice thought. It is comforting to believe that on Christmas Eve others were pleased at the prospect of humanity's newborn chance at salvation, Jesus the Lord.

The angels sang and shepherds adored. Why did the Lord come to shepherds above all the rest of humankind on that Christmas Eve? The answer is that he did not. God is present to all humans at every moment of their lives. He speaks to every human at every moment, but only some humans listen and only some humans act on the message heard.

God came to the shepherds through angelic choirs, and perhaps that dramatic method was an advantage (though even the dramatic can be discounted if we try hard enough); but he came to others in other ways, ways that were best suited to them as individuals. The song of angels moved the shepherds to belief and action because they were prepared to believe and act. They responded to the song by saying: "Let's take a chance! Let's set aside our usual occupation; let's change our lives and go over to Bethlehem and see if we can find this God-child." Find him they did, and as Luke reports (2:18-20), they "returned, glorifying and praising God for all they had heard and seen, . . . All who heard of it were astonished at the report given them by the shepherds."

We don't know what happened to the shepherds after that. We don't know if the coming of the Lord to the shepherds on that one occasion changed their lives forever, whether or not they dedicated themselves to do God's will for the rest of their lives. Probably not. Only Mary and John the Baptist were that firm in their commitment throughout a lifetime. Most of us poor humans need the Lord to come again and again to us to keep us from making eternal fools of ourselves. Seeing God once, we have a momentary high, but then, need the quiet action of God's grace to keep us from going off the deep end, believing that finally and forever we are saved and will never again be conquered by a temptation to ignore the Lord or disobey his will. Having seen God, we need the grace of God to prepare us for his next coming (which may not be as "pretty" as the Christmas-Child). The shepherds, who were young enough and were "converted" by the pleasing infant in the crib, would need great grace to stand seeing the end of this infant, twisted and deformed on a criminal's cross.

Still, there is a good chance that those shepherds did finally succeed in making it to the heavenly banquet. On at least one occasion they had shown the energy to go out of their way to see the Lord. Perhaps this was the beginning of a habit that would bring them back to the Lord again and again throughout their lives. If so, no matter what else happened to them in the interim, in the end they joined their angelic friends at the banquet of the Lord.

## *"What," "Where," "Why": A Christmas Eve Reflection*  28

In trying to make sense of Christmas we must answer three questions, two of them easy and one of them hard.

The first question is simply "What happened?" With faith the answer is clear. On that first Christmas the God who holds the universe in the palm of his hand was born of a virgin, a human being like us in every way except sin. It is an event that is easy to state but impossible to understand. In the words of Augustine:

> Christians, let us celebrate the Lord's human birth when he became one of us that through the invisible made visible we might be able to move to the invisible from the visible. . . . This birth from a virgin is unexplainable. Who can understand this strange, extraordinary happening . . . this event unique in the history of the world? What human reason does not grasp, faith accepts. Where reason fails, faith succeeds. For who would say that the Word of God who made all things could not have taken flesh? (Sermon 190, no. 2)

God became a human being: this we Christians believe. But where do we hold this belief? As I write these words I sit in a room on a pleasant college campus just outside of Philadelphia in the state of Pennsylvania in the United States of America. This country is one small part of a massive planet that we call the earth. The earth itself is only one of several planets (most of them much larger) that spin around a huge ball of fire called the sun, a ball of fire which luckily is ninety-three million miles away from us in that exact spot conducive to human life on earth. This sun that seems so awesome is really only a minor star in a cluster of stars called the Milky Way, a galaxy containing some hundred billion stars with the nearest more than six trillion miles away. Our galaxy is only one of a thousand million galaxies, each with hundreds of billions of stars. And still, with all these planets and stars and galaxies, the universe in which we work out our brief lives on earth is mostly empty space.

This is the place where we live. This is the place where God became human: a minor planet in a minor system of a minor galaxy of a universe whose magnitude exceeds our powers of imagination. This God who became human with us is the God who holds the unimaginable universe in the palm of his hand, like the shimmering glass ball filled with snowflakes that we give to our children on Christmas morning.

The third question about Christmas is the most difficult of all: "Why would God become a human being?" Thinking about this mystery Augustine remarked:

> "God's power is indeed a source of wonder but we should marvel even more at his mercy . . . that he who was able to be born as a human being would *want* to be born as a human being." (Sermon 192, no. 1)

The only answer that can be given to the question: "Why?" is that God *wanted* to become human, and the only explanation for this *wanting* is love. Because he loved us, he did not want us to be condemned to live forever in the everlasting darkness that is the universe without him. God came to our place because he wanted to take us home some day to his place. God wanted to live our life so that someday we could live his. God wanted to live our life so that he could die our death and thereby save us from ourselves. God became a human being because he wanted to give us hope.

This message of hope has been proclaimed by Christianity for over two thousand years. It is the message that Augustine preached to his congregation in the year 400:

Awake humanity! For your sake God has become a human! "Awake you who sleep, rise up from the dead, and Christ will enlighten you!" (Eph 5: 14) I say again: "For your sake, God became human!" (Sermon 185, no. 1)

It is the message of hope that still warms our hearts today as we spin out our lives on this minor planet, twirling through the darkness of a universe beyond our comprehension.

# PART II

# The Twelve Days of Christmas: "The Lord Has Come!"

# A Child Has Come                                    29

The angels sang: "A child has come! Let the Earth rejoice!" (Luke 2:11) There is a great mystery here, and a great truth.

The truth is that it is easy to rejoice over newly born children. Babies are loved mostly, and it is a dark mystery of human perversity when they are not. Babies are needed. The human race could not get along without babies, at least not for very long. Augustine even said that babies were the best proof that God still loved the human race after the disaster of Eden. All things considered, babies are fine people. They don't make wars. They don't cheat in the stock market. They are not fickle in their love. Babies come highly recommended. Why, I was one myself, and so were you, and so was the Lord Jesus. Herein lies the mystery.

Why in the world would the Lord of the universe want to begin his earthly career as a baby? If it were up to me to decide my beginning, I would opt to be an emperor—or at very least a full professor. If I had my way, I would want to begin my life with tenure, not tenuously like a baby. A baby doesn't have much say about its early years. It is powerless. It lives dependent on the kindness of others. Babies are nice people mostly, but they are no great shakes in changing the course of history. In terms of this world's power structure, babies are at the bottom of the ladder. Why in this world would Jesus want to start that way? It is a great mystery.

Perhaps some day he will let us know the reasons. Just now we can only guess. Who knows? He may have come as a baby because he wanted to have a complete experience of both the bad and the good in human life—like the son of the president of the company, starting his career by sweeping the floors. Jesus may have wanted to bear our birth and live our life and die our death so that thereafter no human could ever turn to him and say: "You just don't understand what I am going through!"

Perhaps Jesus wanted to begin as a baby so that he could experience the great good things of being a baby (experiences that old pots like me and you have long since forgotten), experiences like seeing light for the very first time, experiences like waking from a good sleep hungry and being fed by someone who obviously loves us. Maybe Jesus began as a baby because he wanted the experiences of being held by a mother and playing innocent games with a father. If he had begun life as an emperor or a full professor, he would have missed all that. Emperors seldom find playmates, I am told, and in my experience there does not seem to be a great rush to cradle full professors in loving arms. They are sometimes tenured but seldom tenderly held in public. As a baby Jesus could play without embarrassment and demand as his due that he be loved—even in public places.

But the most cogent reason for Jesus' beginning this life as a baby was that he wanted to keep before our eyes a memory of what our future would be like. We cannot go back to our beginnings on this earth, but one day we shall be born into the next life. On that great day we shall once again experience the amazed wonder, the unconditional trust, the easy laughter of our baby days. Once borne again into heaven, the wonder and trust and laughter will never end.

## A Family Celebration* 30

When Jesus was born, the only things he had going for him were his family and his divinity. Oddly enough, his being God was little help in his human adventure. He had decided not to make much of his "being God," and thus throughout his earthly life he was treated like any other poor human. We are told that he "emptied himself" so that he could have the full experience of being human, the bad parts as well as the good parts. One of the good parts was in having a family.

Jesus chose to be a member of a human family. He knew it was not an unmixed blessing. He knew from the beginning what we learn only after a period of time: living in a family is not all sweetness and light. There are special fears and tears and frustrations in family living. We are loved more deeply and also hurt more deeply by family than by strangers. We worry about losing family more than losing acquaintances. The guilt of failing one's family is the worst guilt of all. But even with these negatives, Jesus still wanted to be part of a human family so that he might enjoy the gifts that only a family can give.

Perhaps Jesus wanted family so that he could have someone to brag about. Joseph, his foster-father, filled the need nicely. As a kid, Jesus probably enjoyed bragging about Joseph—about how strong he was, about the fine carpenter he was. Jesus may have shown his friends the little toys Joseph made for him on his birthdays. He may have stood on the street corner with his friends and claimed: "My father can beat your father." Joseph was strong enough to found the claim, and Jesus was kid enough to make it.

Perhaps Jesus wanted family because he wanted the experience of having a mother. He probably knew the truth that Thomas Aquinas would write down centuries later, the truth that mothers make the best lovers. Of course, this is not verified in every instance. Some mothers don't want their children. Jesus may have worried about this and thus first asked Mary if she would mind being his mother. Jesus never goes where he is not welcome. Happily, Mary did welcome him, and he came into this world as her son. He must have been happy, too, because he gave her great gifts for saying yes.

Jesus got his family. Like us, he was born in a family way. It was one of the good elements in his human life, just as it is for most of us. There were sorrows of course, but with the strength that comes from family, the sorrows were endured. Jesus was able to bury Joseph and still get on with life. After Joseph's death he was able to take over the task of supporting himself and his mother. He was able to overcome the sadness at not being able to provide for her as he would like. He was able to handle the pain of having to leave her alone to get on with his mission in life. He was able to choke back his anger at those other relatives who did not seem to care a "fig" for him or his mother. The only time they took interest in him was when he came back to preach to them. They wanted to kill him then, and probably some of them made up part of the crowd that crucified him later on. If Jesus got great consolation from being a family man, he also got his fair share of grief.

And yet, when he died, he must have been glad that he had a family. His last dim vision in death was of that same woman who first held him at birth. Being in a family helped him to live and helped him to die. Even that part of his family that killed him at least gave him human roots. He could point to them and say: "These people are mine."

On the cross he said that about all of us. He thought of us and said to his mother: "Here are your children! From now on they are family."

And thus it is that Christmas is a family celebration for all of us. Every human being can celebrate the birth of that Jesus who is our brother. Every human being can look forward to the day when we shall join him and his mother and all the saints in heaven, where finally and forever we shall be at home with our flesh and blood.

*The substance of this theme was first published in *The Bible Today*, "Reflections for December–January," 22, no. 6 (November 1984) 350–52.

## *Appearance and Reality*                        31

Christmas reminds us that we cannot always judge reality from appearances. The young can have wisdom beyond their years. The old can be truly young in heart and spirit. A beautiful facade can mask emptiness within. Ugliness can hide a beauty beyond compare. Human flesh can contain the divine.

One clear message of Christmas is that appearances can be deceiving. It is an important message for many of us who spend so much time doing things for appearances' sake: trying to achieve a beauty beyond our capabilities, grasping at the symbols of power, gathering "things" to symbolize our success at playing the game of life.

Symbols are not bad in themselves. It depends on how we use them. Sometimes they can be used to oversimplify reality. We paint evil as a snake; we paint good as someone just like ourselves. Our country is a proud eagle; the enemy is a cruel bear. What we don't like is painted ugly; what we do like is painted pretty.

Sometimes our symbols perform a positive service, capturing a reality we cannot describe in words. We paint our love as a pounding heart. We paint our mind as a brilliant light. We paint our sanctity as an ethereal halo. But how shall we paint our God?

Scripture tells us. It says that if we are to paint our God, we should paint him as a helpless baby lying in a crib. We should picture him as a child lost on its way to the Temple. If we must picture our God, we can picture him as a carpenter of no great wealth. If we must have pictures to remember our Incarnate God, Jesus Christ, we should paint him as a teacher who thought that ordinary folks were blessed. We should paint him as an innocent victim of human perversity, one who submitted to death so that he could save his executioners.

The Bible tells us that this is how Jesus Christ appeared to be and then goes on to insist that his reality is much, much more. The true glory that is Jesus-God is more than our poor human minds can imagine. On the first Christmas only a very few were able to get beyond appearances to see that glory. And so it has been ever since.

Our faith tells us that God lives in our world today as truly as he lived in the Christmas stable of Bethlehem. The only difference is in the appearances that hide him. God lives; he is there just below the appearances of ordinary life. He is deep below those surface things that we use to describe and define ourselves. He has come and will continue to come to us as we make our way through this life.

Christmas proclaims that God has already found each one of us. Our task now is to find him behind that world of appearances that consumes so much of our daily lives.

## *Christmas in the Hospital*                    32

It is hard to be in the hospital at Christmas time, but that is where we are. Our life is lived in a hospital, or at least a hospice—a care-facility for those who are terminal. This analogy is not new. Augustine described human history as the period when the dying are constantly ceding their beds to the newly born. (*City of God*, bk. 15, ch. 1) It is almost as though there are only a certain number of beds on this earth, and new admissions cannot be processed until some of us are released to that great world beyond the doors, where we shall dance in good health with the Lord, our good doctor.

Christmas brings a special loneliness to those confined in hospitals and nursing homes. Any patient who can muster the strength is released, leaving behind the poor folks who simply cannot exist outside. Patients who go home for Christmas are able to pretend and hope that they are doing well. Those who remain behind cannot escape the conviction that their condition is serious.

Being in the hospital at Christmas is difficult for the staff too. There are no miracles of healing attempted during holidays. Efforts are directed to "holding the ground" until after the holidays. Both patients and staff are glad when normal activity returns and they can get on with treating and being treated—with their fight for life, their need to die.

On Christmas Day only emergencies are handled in our hospitals: those who simply insist on being admitted or being born, those who simply insist on exiting through death. Few volunteer for hospital duty on Christmas Day. Visitors come and go hurriedly, anxious to get on with their celebrations outside. You really can't blame them. Who wants to care for the sick on Christmas Day?

Only Jesus-God. The wonder of Christmas is that Jesus chose to be born to us in this hospital that is our world. He did it freely. He did it lovingly. He did not want us to be alone in the fears and pain and tiredness that sometimes go with being alive in this place for healing.

His coming *does* change things. It does make us feel better. It is not so bad being in a hospital when you know that the Lord walks the corridors. He does not always cure us right away, but we don't feel so much alone with him on the premises. And he promises that someday we shall be cured, that someday we shall be born into his life as he was born into ours. He promises that someday he will help us get *out* of this hospital. Meanwhile he will help us get *through*. Knowing the Lord has come to heal us is a source of joy even on a Christmas Day in the hospital. We *are* in a weakened condition. What better place is there than this place for healing where the Lord God is the chief resident?

## *A Christmas Balloon*  33

It is only hard being human when you think about it. Sometimes we survive by "not-thinking" (living Unamuno's gloomy assertion "Consciousness is a disease!"). What we are trying to avoid thinking about is the fragility of our lives and the dangerous seasons that we must survive.

We don't mind fragility as long as it does not happen to us. Children, for example, just love balloons. They are so pliant! They must be filled with air and held, otherwise they die. If the precious wind that gives them substance and form is not pinched in, there is a rush of air, and the poor balloon rushes hither and yon looking for rest. The child laughs as the fragile thing rushes to the heavens only to plummet to the earth. Its wild gyrations are unforeseen and hence amusing. It makes a funny sound as it spins about. The child does not realize that it is the balloon's death rattle.

But then it is not all that bad. The balloon is not necessarily over and done with. The child can blow it up again if the balloon can be found and if the child cares to blow it up and if the balloon is not so old that its wasted skin can no longer hold the breath of life. This last condition is a sad condition for any balloon. After a life of making children happy and being the center of festive celebration, every balloon comes to a point when it can no longer contain life. It is hard to believe it when we see merry balloons in the prime of their days. They seem so bright, so permanent. If we look at them more closely, we realize that even from their first expansion there is a gradual emptying. Every balloon that shares our celebrations is slowly but inevitably losing the precious air that keeps it alive in this world—and so too are we.

Scientists tell us that we are mostly water and air tenuously contained by skin. From our first moment of life outside the womb, our physical well-being depends on our ability to draw new life into our lungs and expel the used air. We are born and we die seeking that precious wind that gives life.

All of our ages are fragile. When we are young and in the springtime of life, we are so small and the world is so large and so strange! We seem to be surrounded by giants. It is so easy to be squashed. We rush to grow bigger, to do something important so that others can see us more easily and not crush us by accident. We yearn for the bright days of our summer life when we shall flourish.

If we are lucky, we make it to our summer in good health and with someone to love us and care for us. We celebrate the fullness of life. Like all balloons we want to "party," and there is nothing wrong with that as long as we do it sensibly. But sometimes we are not sensible. We move from spring's fear to summer's folly. We give up thinking about past and future. Our life-air is so easy to come by! We do not worry about our fragility. It is summer and we are strong! Who needs to pray in the midst of the hot, bright days of August? We enjoy our lives and do not worry about making sense of them. We enjoy our summer days and ignore the inevitable autumn season that will soon come.

Autumn is not necessarily a terrible time. In the early days of our autumn the colors of our lives can peak, drawing people to wonder at our brilliance. It is a time for harvest, when we can reap the crops of love and ambition so laboriously worked in earlier seasons. But autumn has its grey times too. There are autumn doubts. Some have no harvest, and for everyone there is always something left undone. For everyone there is the nagging question: "What is the meaning of any life if winter is sure to come?" What is the sense of being a glorious balloon if one's life-wind must inevitably dissipate in the cold of winter's sleep?

But then, need winter-sleep be so distressing? When a balloon explodes, its spirit is freed to join the infinite air above. Its disappearance is a victory more than a defeat. Of course it does not know its future. We humans do. We can see the gradual darkening and shortening of our winter days. But then, darkness is not always an evil. We spend half our lives seeking the rest that sleep brings, and we consider ourselves fortunate if we can gently drowse our way into a new day. We do not fear the darkness of a New Year's Eve if we know that we shall indeed awake to a new year with its promise of a new spring.

We fragile humans would not fear the windless sleep of death if we knew *for certain* that we would be filled again with refreshing air, that someone somewhere would someday fill us again with the sweet spirit of life.

Here in the north we are fortunate in having Christmas come in the midst of winter darkness. It reminds us that fragile days can sometimes give birth to wondrous events. The fragility of the Christmas Child testifies to the eternal security of humans. Christ becoming human shows that all of our human seasons, fragile though they may be, have an infinite worth. The Infinite has chosen to take them to himself. The message of hope is clear: If the infinite Lord cares that much about fragile humanity, is it too much to believe that he will fill us forever with his divine breath?

He *said* that he would. He *promised* that he would. The words are there in the Book of Ezekiel (38:12, 14):

Thus says the Lord God: "O my people, I will open your graves
and have you rise from them . . .
I will put my spirit in you that you may live . . .
I have promised, and I will do it."

It is a fine promise for any balloon or any human being.


*Sunrise: Sunset*                                    34


Dawn and dusk are beautiful on some days when the condi-
tions are just right. Whether the sun is on its way to visit my day
or whether it is departing to dance in the day beyond my horizons,
the colors are often magnificent. Indeed, the moments of dawn and
dusk are some of the most beautiful moments of life and also some
of the most hopeful.

At dawn I look forward to the new bright day that has been
given to me. At dusk I rest and look forward to the light of the
new day soon to come. In the midst of my dawns and dusks I stand
quietly on my little piece of earth and wonder at the beauty of a
universe painted with the colors of God's sun. I celebrate my life
during my earthly dawns and dusks.

I also celebrate my life at the seasons that commemorate the
dawn of God's Son here in my world and that final dusk when I
shall go with the Son to his. At Easter I celebrate the resurrection
promised by the departing Son of God. I am happy as the shadows
deepen in my life because I know that soon I shall follow the wild
brilliance of that Son as he leads me beyond the horizon to that
world where there is no dawn or evening—only the pure light of
an infinite God.

At Christmas I celebrate the coming of that same Son into my
earthly life—a truly unexpected event! The chosen people of Israel
prayed that God would come to rescue them, to lead them to a better
life. They did not dream that God's Son would come and *share* their

life, that he would *endure* their days with them, that he would *stay with them* as the night of death approached, that he would carry them through that dusk to a new and eternal dawn. They could not *imagine* that the Son would come and become *involved* with them. But that is exactly what Jesus Christ did then and now does for each one of us. And so, on Christmas we *all* can celebrate the coming of the Son to our earthly lives.

On some mornings it is hard to see the sun, but even on the darkest morning we still know that it is there. We are sad that it is not shining brightly, but we are thankful that there is *some* light. We know that soon the clouds will clear and that our days will become bright and warm again. We have hope because we know that the sun is with us, nourishing and supporting us, even though just now we cannot see it.

And so it is with our lives. In our gloomy times, when the light is dim, we should remember the message of Christmas:

The dawn has come! The Son is with us even now! Even now we run with him through our earthly hours towards that eternal day that has no dusk!

## *A Lighthouse Christmas*          35

Once on a Christmas past I sent my friends a card with a picture of a lighthouse on the front. They may have been expecting a picture of the nativity scene or of the shepherds in the hills or even a picture of a star, but I sent them a picture of a lighthouse instead. A lighthouse on a Christmas card? How odd! But what do you expect from a simple professor? One of the joys of full-time teaching of philosophy is that eccentricity is allowed, if not positively expected. And yet I do believe that I had some good reasons for my lighthouse card.

First, the picture was of one of my very favorite spots. It was a winter photograph of the Nubble Light, a lighthouse situated on a tiny island just off a nub of Maine above York. During my New England years I spent many hours, sometimes alone, sometimes with a friend, sitting on the rocks looking out at the silent lighthouse. I never saw the folks who lived there, but once I saw a happy dog romping on the summer grass and knew that they were kind. And once I saw a wash hanging on the line and knew that they were people of hope. A world that does its wash is a world that has not despaired. My only direct evidence of the human spirit dwelling there was when I returned one evening to find the great light shining brightly, crying out over the dark roiling sea, "Here I am! Here I am!"

I liked the card too because it seemed to symbolize my present condition, a somewhat hoary island with a broadening base and a head increasingly mottled by bare spots showing through snowy strands. The seas still roll around my life, but I am somewhat secure, remembering the past storms I have survived. Like a sunny winter's day on the shores of Maine, there is a brilliance in my life despite the sometime cold. As the evening of my life deepens, my lamp is still lit; and I can see other lights shining in response, saying, "I know you live, and I care!"

I believe that my sturdy Maine lighthouse symbolizes other human lives too. We are all lighthouses in our own way, shining away on an island all our own. Perhaps others are *with* us on the narrow island of our history, but even our most precious loves cannot be *in* us. There is a place inside each one of us that no other human can see or share, a house of life and light that is ours alone. It is in this house that we love and hope and dream. It is in this island that we shall eventually die.

Despite that inner "aloneness," our lives are not necessarily lonely or sad. On our external island of shared experiences there are good times. Sometimes the seas are quite calm and the sun is warm and we are with those we love and they are happy. But no season is forever. Our loved ones pass on, and summer plans are covered by winter snows. It is then that the light that still burns within our house cries out most fervently: "Here I am! Is there no one who will stay the night with me?"

The message of Christmas is simply this: Christ has come not simply to our island but into our very house, and no matter how raging the storms, we shall never ever be alone again. Christmas has come to the lighthouse, and our life should now shine with joy. As our light flickers and weakens in this life, we have but to look over the horizon to see the Beacon of Light himself crying: "Here I am! Come to me! You are saved! Finally and forever you are saved!"

## *The Gift of Time*                                          36

As we wait for Christ to come to us in our earthly lives, it is good for us to remember the great mystery revealed in the coming of Christ at that first Christmas so long ago. The mystery is simply this: God has time for each one of us.

"God is willing to give us the time of day!" It is truly a wonderful revelation. Time is the greatest gift given to any of us. The worst insult one can give to another is to say (by words or action): "I have no time for you!"

Christmas is the season that reminds us that God has time for us. How sad it is that at Christmas we do not always make the same gift to each other. We substitute things for our time. We send Christmas cards printed by machine so that we will not need to waste time writing our name. We buy present after present for our kids, hoping that they will know that we love them even though we can spend little time with them. We are encouraged to buy fancy watches for loved ones to prove we love them, forgetting that someone who measures our love by a "watch" is not worthy of our time.

On the first Christmas there were no gifts at all, only people who loved each other. God came to visit with us poor humans ("naked we enter life and naked we will depart"), and poor shepherds came to visit an infant God. There were no watches exchanged, only time and love.

Jesus became human so that he could win back eternity for us by his sacrificial death, but before that terrible event took place he spent time living with us through ordinary days.

> He spent time playing with children.
> He took a day off to spend time with a businessman, Zacchaeus.
> He spent time with the sick and disabled . . . curing them by his interest.
> He spent time with the sinful . . . forgiving their sin, curing their blindness.
> He spent time weeping for a dead friend.
> He gave time to his sometimes stupid disciples.

He had only thirty-three years of time on earth, and he did not consider any time he gave to a human being to be a waste.

As we rush here and there during our time of waiting for the Lord, we should remember that the most precious gift we can give to our loved ones is our time. And in giving of ourselves to those who need us, we are giving to God. He tells us: "As often as you give time to a human in need, you give time to me."

God has come into our times so that we might be able to go with him into eternity. Even now he is with us through our good times and bad times, gently drawing us to that final rest. No human needs to give an expensive watch to God to be sure of his love. All any of us need do is spend a little time with him in this life. All we need do is spend a little time with those fellow humans who need us. We must give time to God and to each other. If we do only that, we shall be loving God above all and loving our neighbor as ourselves. If we do only that, God will be with us in all our present times and in that eternity that is our future.

## Celebration of Our Time 37

On New Year's Eve many humans have the time of their lives (or so they claim; we who are "long in the tooth" have a tendency to have our toasts with Maalox at eight o'clock and fall into our bed exhausted). On New Year's Day all of us, young and old, are invited to *celebrate* the times of our lives. New Year's Day is about the only holy day on which we celebrate time. It is therefore an appropriate time to think about the mystery of our time.

The first thing to be said is that our time moves in a straight line. What is past is past and cannot be repeated or changed. What is future is ahead of us and for the most part is hidden from us. We know exactly what happened to us last year (bad and good) and cannot change it. It is part of our history, part of the story of our lives. We do not know what will happen to us in the coming year exactly, and we do not have complete control over it. It may be the year when we will fall in love, or find a friend, or get sick, or die.

The nature of our time combined with the teachings of Christ teaches several important lessons. First, we must learn from our past but not try to relive it. Second, we must move forward into the future and not be afraid of it. And why? Because Jesus Christ has come into our time and will be with us now in this life through whatever time is given to us.

We are destined to go through many stages of life if we live long enough. We are born, we grow, we flourish, we grow old, we die. Such is the pattern of our lives, and no matter how long the time we have, it is not a long time if it comes to an end. Compared with eternity, every life is short. In light of the eternity before us the crucial question becomes: "Can I live with myself until I die and ensure that I will live with God thereafter?"

The response of faith is that I will be able to live with myself if now in my present I do not act in such a way that I will create a past that will torment me with guilt. I will be able to live happily forever if now in my present I try to do my best to love God above all and my neighbor as myself. If I can do only that in any new day given to me, then that day will indeed be a fruitful day for time and eternity.

I am old enough (and functioning enough) to remember the days of Rudy Vallee. In his heyday (before being put out to pasture), he made famous the song "Your Time Is My Time."

This is the song that Jesus Christ sings to humanity. God took upon himself human nature in the person of Jesus Christ and thereby took upon himself all the times of our lives:

. . . the time of being born helpless
. . . the time of feeling the strength and vigor of youth
. . . the time of experiencing human love
. . . the time of feeling the roll of time rushing past as one tries to accomplish some great work in life.
. . . the time of idle hours as others waste our time.
. . . the time of hoping for a time of suffering to pass quickly and not having it happen.
. . . facing the time of death with anxiety.
. . . plunging through the moment of death with a sigh of relief: "It is finished."

Jesus came into our time so that we might not be alone in living out the times of our lives—past, present, future. He came into our time so that we might live knowing that our past is forgiven, our present is filled with the presence of God, and our future is held in the hands of Infinite Love.

Believing this, we can be happy through all the rest of the times of our lives.

# *The Tire Rolls On:* *A New Year's Reflection*                      38

This season is a time for endings and beginnings. The cycle of my years rolls on. Another revolution has been completed. Year follows year, cycle after cycle, like a wheel spinning on an automobile plodding through time. I feel like the tire, gradually losing my tread as I spin into the future.

As I get older, one year seems much the same as the one past. Shadow follows light. Light follows shadow. Spring green is followed by summer's hazy blue. Autumn brown quickly goes to winter white. There is momentary darkness and then spring reappears. Season follows season as I spin through birth and adolescence and youth and middle age and then old age. Each year has its peaks and valleys, and as I travel through my history the only real change seems to be in *me* as I wear down, my life becoming a finer and finer fabric. I know that inevitably there will be a puncture in my flimsy surface and my life-spirit will rush out leaving nothing but worn-out remains, or so it seems as I look back.

My faith allows me time for remembering, but it encourages me to spend more energy on my future. The Scripture reading appropriate for the new year is the opening passages of the Gospel of John where he speaks about that beginning before time itself. In that beginning (he says) there was God. The message of the chapter is that God was then, is now, and ever shall be. God is in my future as much as (and even more than) he was in my past. I may feel diminished with the passage of time, but God does not become less. I am a year older, but Jesus Christ is still growing in me.

It is a consoling thought for an old tire worn down by the passage of many years. It reminds me that I am still alive in this new year and that eternal happiness is still possible for me. God is even now in this world fighting to make my salvation a reality. As John says: "God is in the world and anyone who accepts him is empowered to become a child of God." God is not behind me. He is in front of me. "The Word has been made flesh and *now* dwells with me."

At the beginning of a new year, my song should not be about "auld lang syne," the good old days long since past. Rather I should sing about the years and eternity that is my future. My future is not to spin through accustomed paths, gradually wearing out like an old tire. My future is finally to break free of the cycle of my years and leap like a silver arrow into eternity, where every moment will be new and filled with the excitement of youth.

## *The Family* 39

Christmas has come and gone. The refuse has been cleaned up. The dishes have been put away. Our broken toys have been thrown out. We begin to think about how to pay the bills. We are back into our comfortable, ordinary, scruffy clothes, looking at another ordinary day of our lives.

The angelic choirs have stopped their singing. All that can be heard is the traffic of an ordinary day on the road outside. The visitors have gone back to their own lives and their own ways. Their good wishes still ring in our ears, but we suspect that some of them will never be seen again. We come to understand that important truth about post-Christmas days: after the guests have gone, there is only family to get us through the rest of our days.

The Holy Family must have experienced that truth on their own day after Christmas. By that time the shepherds were long gone, back to the duties of their shepherding. The sound of singing angels was only a memory. The only sounds to be heard were the ordinary animal noises of the other guests in the stable. The Holy Family was in a posture of adoration for only a brief time. When the sun rose on the new day, Joseph had to begin worrying about where the next meal was to come from. He was unemployed and needed a job. Mary had to take care of the baby and clean up the stable a bit. She also had to think of a more permanent residence for their stay in Bethlehem. A stable is no place to care for a child. On the day after Christmas, the wonder of it all probably dimmed a bit, as they began to think about how to get through the rest of their lives.

As far as we know, they did not get any special help from God or human beings in their effort to find a livable place and to make a living. The times were hard and they were poor. The only thing they had going for them was that they were family—a community of humans bound by love. This was all they had and it was all they needed. They did not need miracles. God had already given them his first and greatest gift for getting through life. He had given them each other bonded together in family.

There is an important message in all of this for every human being. God gave us Jesus so that we could be redeemed. God gave us Christmas so that we could have a day of celebration. But God gave us family to get through the ordinary days of our lives—the good days and the bad days when nothing much is happening or when we feel very much alone.

The one security we can have in life is to have someone that truly loves us—one who is part of us in blood, flesh, and spirit. With family, we can know that there is always a place for us to go when we want to celebrate. With family, we can know that there is always a place to call when we need help.

Jesus wanted to have family because he knew that it was the only way for an ordinary human to make it through life. He wanted to have a family because he wanted to have that highest experience of human love possible to any human being, the pure self-sacrificing love found in the good family.

No matter who we are or what we have accomplished in this life, in the end the only thing that will be important to us is family.

If we are lucky, we will end our lives knowing that there are some humans who love us and who will mourn our passing.

If we are lucky, we will end our lives with those who love us with us in our dying.

If we are lucky, we will remember that God has made us part of his family. He has adopted us as sons and daughters and sent his only natural Son to us on Christmas so that he might be with us in life and death.

If we are lucky, we will remember that we are family with God and that he is even now calling us to come home to him, where finally and forever we shall be united with our flesh and blood, Jesus Christ, the Lord.

## *After the Coming*                                        40

The Lord has come: so what else is new? Jesus has been born into this world and has come into individual human lives. What difference does it make?

A friend of mine told me about the fears of her little daughter. The girl was suddenly very afraid of death. She said: "They tell me that there is a heaven, but I can't be sure!" She was truly frightened by the uncertainty of this life, this life that is lived after the coming of the Lord. She believed that the Lord had come, but this did not take away her fear of death, nor does it for most of the rest of us.

What, then, does the coming of the Lord do for us in our daily lives? One thing for sure—it does not take away the troubles. The feasts that follow Christmas make that very plain.

The very day after Christmas we celebrate the Feast of St. Stephen, the first martyr. The coming of Jesus did not save Stephen from execution. The human prejudice that killed Stephen was not lessened by the Lord's coming. The Lord's coming gave the human race another reason to be prejudiced and fearful. It formed another camp of humanity ("those Christians") who could be hated and persecuted.

On the day after St. Stephen's feast, we celebrate the Feast of St. John, the one apostle who lived to be an old, old man. The coming of Jesus did not cure John of the aches and pains of being old. There is a tradition that at the end of his life he had to be carried from place to place, so decrepit was he. This "son of thunder" ended up as a whisper. He must have wondered why God stuck him on this earth so long. He wanted to go home. All of his friends had gone. Mary had gone. Jesus had come and gone. John was left to live as a leftover of a generation that had gone to dance and sing in a better place. The coming of the Lord to John did not take away the burden of his old age.

After John we commemorate the Holy Innocents, those children who were summarily executed because of an ambitious king's fear.

The violence that took the lives of those babies was not prevented by the coming of the Lord. The coming of the Lord does not cure the madness in humanity which makes us kill and kill and hate and hate for no good reason. The presence of the Christ-Child on this earth did not eliminate terroristic acts. It was the occasion for one.

It seems that the Lord has come and gone, he comes and goes, and the quality of human life is not improved at all. We still fear death. We still are prejudiced. We are still liable to end our lives sick and alone. We still kill innocents. What change has the coming of the Lord made in human life, in my life and your life?

The answer is simply this: while not eliminating all the bad times of our lives, the coming of the Lord helps us live through them. It does so by giving us two assurances. First, we are no longer alone. The reason why Jesus-God became human was that we were here. He would have come to us individually if each of us had been the only human alive. He wants to walk with us as individuals in much the same way as he walked with the first man and first woman in Eden. This is the message that the old man John left with his followers when he wrote: "What we have seen and heard we proclaim in turn to you so that you may share life with us. This fellowship of ours is with Father and with his Son, Jesus Christ." (1 John 1:3) John is saying that we are *family* with one another and with God. This is the second assurance given us by the coming of the Lord: we are *family*. We are tied to others even when we are most lonely and alone. There is a bond between ourselves and our God and with all those who have loved us, even those who have gone before us in death. We have become children of God: this is what the coming of Jesus tells us. We are going to live forever: this is the reason he became human, so that he could tell us this truth face to face. With a little help from those around us, especially those who believe with us in God's love, the turbulent days of life this side of death *can* be endured. HE is with us. He has come to help us run the rest of the course of our lives. This is the meaning of his coming, and in truth, it makes a *big* difference in the prospects that lie before us.

# PART III

# Epiphany:
# Bringing the Lord to the World

# Epiphany: God's Secret                              41

Jesus came to this world to reveal a great secret, and he began its revelation when he called those three mysterious strangers from the East to visit with him when he was yet a baby. The Epiphany scene preaches his great secret by action rather than words, and the secret is simply this: there are no "foreigners" in God's eyes. There is no chosen people; all humans have been chosen by God to be members of the same body and the sharers of the same promise. There are no outsiders or insiders; there are only the people that God loves.

Before the coming of Jesus, the equal value of all humans was not all that clear. It seemed as though God loved one people more than another. There was a "chosen people," that people which was to produce the Messiah, and it seemed as though God paid special attention to their welfare. He chose their kings, listened to their priests, and spoke to them through his prophets.

The secret of God revealed at the Epiphany was that though the Messiah, Jesus Christ, was *from* the Jewish people, he was *for* all the people. God's secret is that in terms of his affection there is no Jew or Gentile, no male or female, no white or black or yellow or red or brown. There is only *humanity* and Jesus, God Incarnate, who comes to make the same promise of eternal life to every member of the species. Thus, Jesus preached to rich and poor, to male and female, to countryman and foreigner. He had dinner with saints and sinners. He fraternized with the disabled, held the young in his lap, and made sure that he saw the ancient Anna and Simeon before they died. His entourage included fishermen and tax collectors, women of some substance and boys still looking to make a mark in life. Pharisees came to him for advice, and Roman officers came to him for help. He was willing to speak to rulers and the ruled, and his message to all was the same: "God has forgiven the human race. All humans are saved." He tolerated every human being, and for this he was executed.

He was executed because although humans are willing to go to heaven with God, they seem bound and determined that some other humans will go to hell. We humans have always had difficulty with tolerance. We seem to enjoy making lists of the good and the bad, "us against them" where "them" is anybody not exactly like "us." We make those *others* second-class members of the human race and persecute them for being different.

We have killed each other for being a different color or nationality, for being too young or too old. We have abused each other for being female or male. We have cursed each other because we did not believe in the God of love in exactly the same way. We have made foreign nations "kingdoms of evil," and in dealing with them we have justified any deceit in peace and any means in war.

Prejudice is a *human* creation, and God's secret revealed in his Epiphany is that such prejudice is simply *insane*. There *is* no chosen people; there *is* no nation of assured virtue. There *is* no evil empire in this world except that which is carried in the silly hearts and clouded minds of each one of us.

We call each other names and fear each other because our limited intelligence prevents us from knowing each other and understanding that we share the same hopes and fears and destiny. In our silliness, we think that we will be safer if another person dies. We can't see that if we don't hang together we are all going to hang separately. We are all in the same boat, and it is a hospital ship.

The secret of Epiphany is that God loves each one of us despite our sometimes craziness. He became human to save *every* human. The fact that he was Jewish and brown-skinned and male and a carpenter was accidental to his task, just as it was irrelevant to the scope of his love.

The secret of God is that he comes to save all humans because every human has an infinite value. Perhaps the sign that we humans have finally understood that secret will be when we begin to treat each other as equal children of God. When we stop sending people to hell, then we will be ready to enter heaven. Because in heaven there will be male and female, Christian and non-Christian, Jew and Gentile, black and white, and red and yellow and brown. In heaven we will still have our differences, but for the first time in our eternal lives it will truly make no difference. Then the banquet will begin. And Jesus will serve the meal. And truly we shall get our *just* deserts.

*Ordinary Days*                                                       **42**

The Lord has come. He is now with us for the rest of our lives if we permit him to stay. We now carry him into the world we face each day. What can we expect from this presence? a continuing party? ecstasy without end? If it happens this way for us, it will be quite unusual.

Even the great saints spent most of their lives getting through ordinary days. After Augustine had used his first thirty years sowing wild oats, he spent the last forty harvesting the fields of the Lord. Most of the time he was bone-tired. He walked with Jesus through his ordinary days as an ecclesiastical administrator knowing more insomnia than ecstasy, more heartburn than heart burning with joy.

The Church itself seems to recognize this predominance of the ordinary in human life. Of the fifty-two Sundays of the year, the Church has designated thirty-three Sundays as Ordinary Time. These are Sundays when nothing special is happening. To these we could very well add the ten Sundays of Advent and Lent, times when we are waiting for something to happen rather than celebrating a happening. Thus, forty-three out of fifty-two Sundays are commemorations of days when there is no great event.

On such ordinary days it is hard to come up with a pious thought—much less a sermon. These are days when it is easier to do the "funnies" than to do theology. On ordinary days we daydream, remembering the good times of the past and hoping for better times in the future. It is not that the present is unpleasant; it is just so *ordinary*. It is hard to define what an ordinary day is (they are so *ordinary*), but we all recognize them when they come along. An ordinary day for me is the first day of class when for the millionth time I say, "Today we begin a new semester. Here is the syllabus. The drop-add ends in ten days." An ordinary day for some is the day you are fourteenth in line at the supermarket with a cart full of melting ice cream and screaming kids. An ordinary day for others is waiting in the cold for the bus or train to take you to work. An ordinary day for the homeless is every day waking to wonder where breakfast will come from. An ordinary day is any day you have a cold.

A life of extraordinary days exists only in TV ads (where everyone seems to be rushing off to have a good time in a new car or rejoicing in the wash or primping for a party). Oh, we do have our share of exceptional days, but most of the days of our lives are just ordinary.

And so too was it with Jesus. He spent three years preaching to people but thirty years living with them quietly at Nazareth— playing with them, going to school with them, working with them, praying with them, celebrating with them, weeping with them. Even in his public life of teaching there were many quiet times. Indeed, the reason why humans crucified Jesus was that his life seemed so *ordinary*, and he claimed to be so *extraordinary*. The people could not believe that God Almighty was *so* interested in ordinary days that he became a human being to have his fair share of them.

But that is exactly what God did. And why? Because he loves ordinary days as much as he loves ordinary people. He *loves* those days because he knows that it is on such days that we, the ordinary folks that he loves, carry him to our world. It is on these days that we have most of our opportunities for acting like decent people, people of faith, people who truly believe that God is in this world and indeed is *in us* as we make our way through the days of our lives.

When the Lord comes to us, he is unlikely to come with trumpets and fireworks. He is likely to come through the people we meet day in, day out: our loves, our children, our parents, our brothers and sisters, the stranger who comes to us for help, the stranger who is kind to us, our enemies.

A philosopher once said that religion is what you do with your solitude. Jesus says that religion is what you do with your ordinary days. Jesus is with us all the time, but he is with us especially on our ordinary days. And so, even on my most pedestrian day of teaching, I should remember that the Lord is reaching through me to my bored audience. As I teach my metaphysics, I have cause to celebrate. God is with me! I just hope I don't fall asleep.

## The Race                              43

The Lord has come. He is now with us for the rest of our lives if we permit him to stay. We now carry him into the world we face each day. What can we expect from this presence? peaceful rest? Far from it. We are in a race, and the only difference that the Lord's presence makes is that now he is running along with us.

From the very beginning of our lives, we are in a race towards our ending. Conception leads inevitably towards death. We run here and there in the course of our living, but wherever we go, we move inevitably towards a common goal. The limits of our race are set. The only question is whether we shall end up as winners or losers. If we meet our death hand in hand and heart in heart with Jesus, then we have won our race no matter what else has happened to us in life.

In the course of our lives, the matter is unsettled. Our early years are somewhat secure. Our lack of responsibility protects us from purposely rejecting the Lord, and thus he stays with us and in us through our days of innocence. His work, then, consists of trying to get us to grow in the knowledge and love of him. The simple faith of the child who comes smiling with its parents to Communion (not yet able to receive but unwilling to be left out) is a sign that Jesus is already in that child.

As we grow out of those innocent years, we sometimes become interested in anything *other* than the Lord. Then he must run after us, trying to bring us back to an understanding of the divine presence in the universe—some power beyond ourselves and better than ourselves to which we must answer for our lives. If we come at least to that, Jesus is satisfied for the moment. We have reached out to hold the hand of a power beyond ourselves, and that gives the Lord an opening to bring us farther. Our hearts have opened to the divine; now he can work to open our minds, so that we come to believe explicitly in the Lord and the message he teaches.

As we grow to take responsibility for the course of our life, the issue of our winning or losing becomes more problematic. Some are like Dismas, knowing the Lord only at the very end. Some are like Augustine, knowing of Christ from an early age, but then forgetting about him or discarding him. They say: "Oh yes, I was raised Christian, but have outgrown it," seeming to say that they have outrun Jesus to move on to something more modern or relevant or exciting or sophisticated. Having been raised knowing him, they wander off seeking their fortune elsewhere. They race along strange paths, with Jesus the pursuer trying to catch them and lead them back to that one path on which they can run with him through life. Jesus not only knows the way; he is the Way. But sometimes we forget that in our search for something or someone to make us feel good right now. Running with Jesus does not necessarily do that. In fact, it is somewhat tiring. It seems so much more pleasant to simply sit down by the side of the road and play with today's toys with passing friends.

If we are faithful to the Lord, we run each day with Jesus towards our death-goal and the eternal prize that lies just beyond. Knowing where we are going does not take away our fear. Often the Lord with us is not a tangible presence, and we would like some confirmation that he is there. We look back and see only one set of footprints traversing our history: our own. Where is Jesus' mark? At such times we need to remember that Jesus is not so much with us as in us, and therefore the marks we leave as we race along are his marks too.

God knows, the way we humans run through life is often squir-
relly and circuitous. We make sense of it only when we look back.
Then we come to understand that our stops and starts, our detours
into strange countries, were used by the good Lord to bring us suc-
cessfully home. True, some of our excursions may have been stupid and some even malicious, but if we have kept ourselves open
to direction (not thinking that WE were the "way and truth and
life"), then the provident God can make use of our wanderings—
perhaps teaching us a lesson about ourselves that we can only learn
from experience, perhaps being instruments of good for the strangers we touch as we wander through foreign lands. Even the prod-
igal son must have been liked by some whom he met in his travels.
Perhaps some of these came to recognize, from his sin and his forgiveness, the meaning of love of father.

It makes little difference where we run in this life as long as,
at the end, we cross death's boundary with Jesus. If at the end we
finally catch up with Jesus, it makes little difference that in the course
of our lives we sometimes did not know (or even care) where we
were going. But that would truly be a miracle: to purposely avoid
him in life and to suddenly embrace him at the moment of death.
It is much more secure to hold him throughout life lest we miss him
at the end.

That would be a shame: to spend our whole life running after
happiness and in the end miss the Lord who is its source.

*Storms*                                              44

The Lord has come. He is now with us for the rest of our lives
if we permit him to stay. We now carry him into the world we face
each day. What can we expect from this presence? fair weather?
calm seas? There is no guarantee. Indeed, if Scripture has any pro-

phetic value for our personal lives, there is a strong indication that sailing with Jesus does not preclude foul weather. A stormy life is no indication that the Lord is absent.

The first Christians were very afraid of storms. Though they lived by the sea and mostly off the sea's harvest, they could not handle its bad weather. One wonders if they were even able to swim. They seemed to expect that their God would always carry them peacefully above troubled waters.

In the New Testament there are two stories about storms at sea. In the first story, (Matt 14; Mark 6; John 6) Jesus was not in the boat at first. When the storm arose, he came to them walking over the troubled waters. The disciples did not recognize their Lord coming to them in the storm. They thought it was a ghost, and for a moment they were more afraid of Jesus than they were of their troubles. Peter asked for a sign, and Jesus told him to come walk with him on the stormy sea. Peter tried but quickly lost faith and began to sink. Jesus knew that Peter was of good heart (just a bit too impetuous), and so he reached down, lifted him up out of the waves, and helped him back into the boat. Then Jesus got into the boat himself, saying to the petrified disciples: "Take courage, it is I. Do not be afraid." But they were, and they did not stop being afraid until the storm stopped.

In the story of the second storm, (Luke 8; Matt 8; Mark 4) Jesus was in the boat asleep when the weather turned bad. First there was an increasing swell. Then came darkness and wind and huge waves breaking over the sides of the boat. Those like Peter, who knew the sea, were concerned; those who were not accustomed to life on the water were terrified. But Jesus continued to sleep.

They called back to him, "Master, wake up! Are you not afraid of the storm?" But Jesus slept on.

They cried out again: "Master, wake up! Are you not concerned for the future of your Church? What will happen to your work if we drown? What would you do without us?" And Jesus continued to sleep.

Finally, they cried, "Master, wake up! We love you and are scared to death! God help us!" And Jesus woke up.

He said to them: "Why were you afraid? Could you not see that

I was with you? Why were you afraid of being lost? Heaven is being with God even on troubled waters. Hell is being alone, even on a peaceful lake."

"Heaven is where I am. What difference if the boat sinks if we are together? For all you know heaven is not on that distant peaceful shore. It could just be that it is at the bottom of the storm-tossed sea. If I am in your heart it is enough." And then Jesus went back to sleep.

There was a third stormy day reported in the New Testament. The disciples were there, and so too was Jesus. It was the day of his execution. On that day the storm did not cease. Jesus sailed through his death, and the disciples lived through it. They seemed to profit from the terrible experience. Thereafter they were not bothered by storms so much. They lived with Christ and died for him. Oh, they were still scared when the storms came. But now they understood that Jesus was with them, and they were happy. They waited patiently with Jesus for the storm to pass. And so it did, eventually.

And so, too, shall be the storms in our life as long as the Lord is in our boat.

# *Joy After the Lord's Coming*   45

The Lord has come. He is now with us for the rest of our lives if we permit him to stay. Now we carry him into the world we face each day. What can we expect from his presence? A different sort of joy? To be sure!

If we truly believe in the presence of the Lord in our lives, if we truly believe that we have the privilege of showing him our world and showing him off to our world, then we must feel a new sort of joy. With the Lord by our side, familiar things take on a new glory. We see the places and people of our usual world in a new way, and they take on a brilliance and a goodness that we never experienced when we were alone.

Augustine described this phenomenon as follows:

> Is it not a common occurrence that when we are showing certain lovely expanses to those who have never seen them before, either in the town or in the country, and which we have been in the habit of passing by without pleasure because we see them often, our own delight is renewed by theirs at the novelty of the scene? And the closer the friendship between them and us, the more this is true, for in proportion as we dwell in them through the bond of love, so do the things which were old become new for us. *Catechizing the Uninstructed* 12, 17 (PL 40, 324)

What Augustine is talking about is the experience of taking your child to the zoo for their first time and seeing ordinary wonders with a simplicity you had long since lost. He is talking about going with a loved one to a quiet beach, visited alone many times before, and seeing the familiar sea for the first time through the eyes of someone with whom you share a heart. He is talking about explaining the universe to a youngster and feeling through that youngster the startled amazement you had long ago, when you were young and the world seemed new.

If, when Jesus comes to us, we accept him as a friend and carry him with us into our usual places to meet our usual friends, they all suddenly become new and wonderful. We get a new perspective on our life, the events and things and people and values that make up our day. They become fascinating for us because we begin to see them for the first time from his point of view.

We see ourselves not as failing animals but as beings of spirit created by a God who loves us, beings of infinite possibilities with an infinite time to realize them. We don't make so much of *ourselves*. We wonder because we are filled with *HIM*.

We see our loves as persons made precious by eternal love, persons who bring us to the infinite by giving us the experience of love, persons whom we are challenged to cherish for all eternity, persons who will live in our hearts forever. Through the eyes of the Lord, we see our human love for what it really is: the seed of our love for the infinite and the instrument through which the infinite lover comes to us.

We see the things of this world as great good things given us by a God who wanted our pilgrim path to be strewn with beauty—sights and sounds and smells that delight—so that we might be happy even as we are on the way. We see these things as hints of the beauty and order that is in front of us. We rejoice in these great good things even as we listen to their song: "Move on! You haven't seen anything yet!"

We see our death as just a door that we must pass through to reach the land of eternal joy, a land where we will be with our loves, divine and human, forever. Though still scared of the process of dying, we approach it with confidence, knowing that it is but a point on a line with no end. We approach death with the conviction that we shall not pass through it alone—that the Lord will be present to us at that last moment of this life, as he has been at every other moment.

St. John sums up our reasons for joy in a letter to his friends. First, our life in this world is now the same as Jesus Christ. (Cf. 1 John 4:17.) We have taken on the life of God himself. He has come to us and is living in us and is walking with us wherever we go. Second, although this life will end someday, seemingly ending our days of victorious living in God with the final defeat of death, the truth is that "Everyone begotten of God conquers the world, . . . you possess eternal life." (1 John 5:4, 13)

But eternity is then; we are now. How can that *then* make us happy *now?* Augustine responds:

> Just now you have some work to do (your living and your dying) but afterwards you will have your reward. But even now your work should not be without joy. You have hope. . . . Your God will come to you and will wipe away your tears. He will replace the bread of your tears with himself. He will feed you himself for all eternity. . . . Have joy in your hope! If your hope is sweet now, how much sweeter will be that reality you hope for! (*Commentary on Psalm 127,* nos. 2-10)

Why should we be joyful? Because the Lord is with us now, and we can show him around the places where we now live. Because the Lord is with us, and if we let him, someday he will show us around the place where he lives. We live with the Lord now and can live with him forever and ever: that's why we should be joyful.

## *Holy Moses!*                          46

It is a very human reaction. The Lord comes to me and says: "I want you to carry me to the world. I want you to proclaim my will to the world. I want *you*." And we respond: "You want *me*, Lord? Holy Moses!"

Our humility, our belief that we are unworthy of being a Lord-bearer, would be quite inspiring if it were not offset by our tendency to act like God with other people and to pretend to be God by making up our own rules of good conduct. But it is human to be afraid to be a messenger of the Lord. It seems so much easier to be indifferent, to be a spectator as God fights to save the world. And so it was with Moses.

The Israelites probably said "Holy Moses" when they learned that he was to be the one to lead them, but they said it as a question: "Holy *Moses*?" Their surprise is not surprising. Moses had quite a checkered career. Abandoned at birth, he was raised by strangers. He fled into the desert as a young man because he had murdered an Egyptian in a fit of anger. He got his first real job as a gift from his father-in-law. He tended sheep and this seemed to fit in well with his noncharismatic personality. He was not a powerful speaker. Indeed, so serious was his stammer that when he went to the Pharaoh to present the case of the Israelites, he let Aaron do the talking.

Moses lived and died as a man of passion and indecision. He broke the first edition of the Ten Commandments, so mad did he get at the partying children of Israel. When the Lord told him to strike the ground once in order to get water, Moses gave the earth an extra lick just to be sure. He seemed to end his life in failure, watching from a hill as everyone else marched happily into the Promised Land.

And yet this was the human being, this was the "cracked pot" that God chose to lead his people, to be a bearer of the Law, to be a messenger of hope. Hearing his story we could well say: "Holy Moses? This Moses was holy?"

Indeed he was. He was chosen to bring God to his world because he was made holy by his humility and repentance. He *knew* he was not much, and he was quick to admit this fact to humans and to God. And when he *did* fail, he was holy enough to return to God and say: "I did not do well, Lord. Let me try again." Moses pretended to be nothing other than what he was (poor old Moses), and God used him to save from exile that people who would be ancestors of Jesus Christ.

God can work with such an honest human and accomplish great things through him. He cannot work with great pretenders—those who spend their lives picking apart the lives of others, making themselves bigger by making others less. But he can work with anyone who says: "Here I am, Lord!—Moses (or Donald or Mary or Joseph or Theresa). Take me and do through me what you will!"

God can make our lives fruitful if we stand before him with honesty and willingness. We should not be frightened by Scripture stories such as the threat of the master (God) to cut down the unproductive fig tree. (Luke 13:6-9) It is clear that God was disgusted with it, not because it failed to produce watermelons but because it failed to be what it was—a fig producer. Perhaps the reason why it did not do what it was made to do was that it was trying to be bigger than other trees. A scrawny fig tree, it pretended to be a majestic oak. The hopeful part of the story is that it was given another chance, a sign that God is influenced by love more than by the "bottom line." No matter how sappy a tree (or human) may be, if it is at least still alive, the Lord is willing to give it one more year, hoeing around its roots to give it air, manuring it to bring it back to its earthy reality, watering it with his grace.

There is no excuse for not at least trying to bring our Lord to our world. To cry "Lord, I am not worthy" and then go back to sleep is false humility. The Lord *knows* none of us are worthy, but if we accept that fact and be what we are (cracked pots struggling to do the right thing), he can work through us to change history.

There is hope. We are alive. If God can make Moses holy, what can he not do for us?

# A Final Word: The Missing Wise Man                    47

The feast of the Epiphany is the feast that closes off our celebration of the coming of Jesus. It begins the days of our "living" with him for the rest of our lives. It reminds us again of the mystery of Christmas—the coming of God to the human race. At the same time it tells us of a new mystery: the coming of three wise men bearing gifts for the child Jesus. We build our Christmas cribs to remind us of both mysteries.

I have noticed a special mystery depicted in the Christmas crib of the university where I serve. Along with the usual cast of characters, there is one jackass and only two wise men.

Now, some may wonder at the presence of the jackass among the sheep and the cows, but that is not a mystery at all. It was probably the beast of burden for the Holy Family. Also, the crib under discussion is in the midst of a university, an environment where the jackass is not an endangered species.

In any case, the presence of a jackass generally needs to be endured more than explained, but the absence of an expected wise man is a more serious matter. What is the message of the missing wise man in the university Christmas crib? Could it be that one poor fellow did not score high enough in the college boards to get on campus? Or did he stop by my philosophy department and lose his way? There are millions of possible explanations for the strange absence, but there is only one explanation.

The message is simply this: THERE IS ROOM AT THE SIDE OF JESUS FOR ANOTHER WISE MAN . . . A WOMAN OR MAN OF WISDOM WHO IS WILLING TO COME TO CHRIST AND OFFER ALL THAT HE OR SHE IS TO HIM.

The gift of self is the only gift that Jesus wants from any human being. It was the gift that he treasured most from those given by the original wise men. They came bearing gifts of gold, frankincense, and myrrh, but Jesus did not want their gifts. He wanted *them*, body and soul, life and love. He wanted *them* and called them from a distant land and led them to his side in a mysterious way. He wanted *them* so that they would come and receive him into their heart and carry him back with them to whatever land their destiny led them.

The open space in the crib is a sign to you and me that Jesus wants *us* to take our place by his side. He wants men and women of wisdom who will come to him and listen to his message of faith and hope and love, that "secret plan" that Paul speaks about in his Letter to the Ephesians. (3:2-3) He wants men and women of wisdom to learn that message and to carry it to the land they face each day.

The mystery of the missing wise man is thus solved. That empty space by the side of Jesus is the space reserved for you and for me. Jesus wants another wise man, and the persons he wants are you and me.

Unfortunately, he does not need any more jackasses. There is one in the Christmas crib already, and in any Christian community one jackass is quite enough.